# Kafka: Toward a Minor Literature

# Kafka

## *Toward a Minor Literature*

## Gilles Deleuze and Félix Guattari

Translation by Dana Polan
Foreword by Réda Bensmaïa

Theory and History of Literature, Volume 30

University of Minnesota Press
Minneapolis    London

The University of Minnesota gratefully acknowledges
translation assistance provided for this book by the French
Ministry of Culture.

Published by the University of Minnesota Press
111 Third Avenue South, Suite 290, Minneapolis, MN 55401-2520
Printed in the United States of America on acid-free paper
Seventh printing 2006

**Library of Congress Cataloging-in-Publication Data**

Deleuze, Gilles.
  Kafka: toward a minor literature.

  (Theory and history of literature ; v. 30)
  Bibliography: p.
  Includes index.
  1. Kafka, Franz, 1883–1924—Criticism and
interpretation. I. Guattari, Félix. II. Title.
III. Series.
PT2621.A26Z67513    1986    833'.912    85-31822
ISBN 0-8166-1514-4
ISBN 0-8166-1515-2 (pbk.)

# Contents

## Theory and History of Literature
### Edited by Wlad Godzich and Jochen Schulte-Sasse

# Foreword
# The Kafka Effect
*Réda Bensmaïa*

Translated by Terry Cochran

> Writing is born from and deals with the acknowledged doubt of
> an explicit division, in sum, of the impossibility of one's own
> place. It articulates an act that is constantly a beginning: the sub-
> ject is *never authorized* by a place, it could never install itself in
> an inalterable *cogito*, it remains a stranger to itself and forever
> deprived of an ontological ground, and therefore it always comes
> up short or is in excess, always the debtor of a death, indebted
> with respect to the disappearance of a genealogical and territorial
> "substance," linked to a name that cannot be owned.
> — Michel de Certeau, *L'Ecriture de l'histoire* (Paris:
> Gallimard, 1975), p. 327

In December 1934, the *Jüdische Rundschau* published an important text on
Kafka by Walter Benjamin, in which we can read these decisive words: "There
are two ways to miss the point of Kafka's works. One is to interpret them naturally, the other is the supernatural interpretation. Both the psychoanalytic and
the theological interpretations equally miss the essential points."[1] In 1974, when
Gilles Deleuze and Félix Guattari devoted a book to Kafka's work, they took
their point of departure from the same principle: one misses the mark in Kafka
either by putting him in the nursery — by oedipalizing and relating him to mother-
father narratives — or by trying to limit him to theological-metaphysical specula-
tion to the detriment of all the political, ethical, and ideological dimensions that
run through his work and give it a special status in the history of literature. At

the least, this initial convergence between Benjamin's approach and that advanced by Deleuze and Guattari seems worthy of note.

When we read each of the studies carefully, we cannot help being struck by the care taken in each case to avoid what might be called a political-ideological *recuperation* of Kafka or, perhaps, to avoid falling back upon what Deleuze and Guattari call a *hard segment*: the binary machine of social classes, sexes, neurosis, mysticism, and so on. In both cases, we find ourselves face to face with the same attempt to avoid making Kafka just another great *litterateur*. Both pinpoint the need to make way for new philosophical, literary, and even psychological categories to come to terms with this unique work and to lead readers out of the impasse created by so many readings of exegesis.

First, let us read and consider what Benjamin would have us think about Kafka: What is the substance of what he says? What is he attempting to have us experience, and not simply interpret or read? What writing machine— already!—does he want to connect us to? Recall that the study begins with a *political* apologue: Potemkin was having a crisis and was therefore inaccessible, but affairs of state were pending. There was a stack of documents that urgently needed to be signed, and the high officials were at the end of their rope; but a junior clerk named Shuvalkin who was informed of the problem took hold of the documents, impassively marched into Potemkin's bedroom, presented the papers to him, and pressed him to sign them. Without blinking—at least, so it seemed—Potemkin signed all the documents presented to him one after the other. Everyone knows what happened: when the high officials finally had the famous documents in hand, they were stupefied to decipher in each instance the name Shuvalkin. Benjamin continues in a way that is highly significant for us:

> This story is like a herald racing two hundred years ahead of Kafka's work. The enigma which beclouds it is Kafka's enigma. The world of offices and registries, of musty, shabby, dark rooms, is Kafka's world. The obliging Shuvalkin, who makes light of everything and is finally left empty-handed, is Kafka's K. (p. 112)

The "reading" that Benjamin proposes for Kafka's work is clear from the outset and is characterized—no less than that of Deleuze and Guattari—by never trying to find archetypes that claim to have "qualified" Kafka's "imaginary" or to interpret his work by moving from the unknown back to the known: the Castle is God, the world of the father, power that cannot be grasped; the cockroach is anxiety, castration, the dreamworld and its multiple metamorphoses, and so forth. But what is still more striking, neither does Benjamin try—he doesn't consider it useful or necessary—to relate Kafka's work to a *structure* with preformed formal oppositions and a signifier of the kind in which "after all is said and done, $x$ refers to $y$"! Not at all. The reading of Kafka both in Benjamin and in Deleuze and Guattari is determined by the prominence they give to a *politics* of Kafka;

but, as Deleuze and Guattari go on to articulate, this politics is "neither imaginary nor symbolic."

In characterizing the hordes of messengers, judges, assistants, intermediaries, and lawyers who haunt Kafka's text, Benjamin never takes refuge behind a symbolic, allegorical, or mythical interpretation: he considers Kafka's ancestors to be the Jews and Chinese of ancient or contemporary history, or even the Greeks, rather than considering Kafka to be the descendant of "Atlases" who would carry the globe of the world on the back of his neck. Refuge behind myth, recourse to myth as the last hope, is radically rejected:

> Even the world of myth of which we think in this context is incomparably younger than Kafka's world, which has been promised redemption by the myth. But if we can be sure of one thing, it is this: *Kafka did not succumb to its temptation.* (p. 117; my emphasis)

Nor would Benjamin have yielded to the temptation to take refuge behind myth; to do so would be to inject mythical meanings into Kafka's work—to say that Kafka is to modernity what classical myth was to traditional society. Benjamin was one of the first "readers" of Kafka to see and then try to show—to demonstrate—that Kafka's work was, from a certain point of view, to be taken literally: in a word, that it functioned on the surface of its signs and that the issue was not—at least, not *only*—to try to interpret it but, above all, to practice it as an experimental machine, a machine for effects, as in physics. Of course, it is a writing machine or a mass of writing machines that are made of assemblages of nouns and effects, of heterogeneous orders of signs that cannot be reduced to a binary structure, to a dominant or transcendental signifier, or ultimately to some phantasm (originary or not).

Benjamin (who was very well acquainted with Freudian psychoanalysis) was able to avoid at every step the "dreary psychoanalytic interpretations" (Deleuze). When he evoked the well-known texts in which Kafka addresses the father, Benjamin immediately showed how close the link is between what Kafka foregrounds about the relation to the Father and a juridical-political "assemblage" that exceeds and determines the father-son relation since time "immemorial" (as he liked to say):

> The father is the one who punishes; guilt attracts him *as it does the court officials.* There is much to indicate that the world of the officials and the world of the fathers *are the same to Kafka.* (p. 113; my emphasis)

Thus, no matter how we approach it—and this is Benjamin's "lesson"—Kafka's work does not lend itself to domestication. It cannot be made into literature in the way one enters into religion. It resists on all levels, and it demands—at every obstacle and disruption that one simultaneously invents and experiences in its unfolding—not merely a new *rhetoric* or a new mode of *reading* but a genuine "traversal of its writing" (Sollers) from which one does not emerge unscathed. It goes without saying that such a change of perspective—not satisfied with reading, one experiences, travels, concretely transforms oneself—cannot be conceived without a radical change in the very nature of the order of signs that is at work in the text. Benjamin had more than an inkling of this decisive aspect of Kafka's work when he attempted to account for the economy of his short stories (for example, the "undecidable," "unfinished" character of his work). Benjamin introduced the important notion of *gesture*. He may have borrowed the notion from Brecht, but for him it referred above all to a space where the subject of the statement and the subject of enunciation can no longer be separated. Benjamin showed that Kafka could well have adopted Montaigne's phrase: "Mon livre et moi ne faisons qu'un." It is impossible to separate the tool from the artisan, the reader as *lexeograph* (Barthes) from the scriptor as *subscriptor*: they are together as machine and rhizome, a network, an entangled knot of movements and stops, of impulsions and immobilizations to experience interminably. They constitute what Deleuze and Guattari call a body without organs, to experience and to deploy, according to the procedures, methods that are always new. Concerning the Kafkaesque gesture (in the medieval sense of the word), Benjamin says:

> Kafka could understand things only in the form of a *gestus*, and this *gestus* which he did not understand constitutes the cloudy part of the parables. Kafka's writings [*Dichtung*] emanate from it. (p. 129)

Nevertheless, Benjamin does not hesitate to advance hypotheses about the "origin" of Kafka's literary "creation" (*Dichtung*). But rather than ascending to some singular—transcendent—figure or signifier, it is a matter of defining a space, a metastable force that does not refer to a subject but designates a *vection*, a movement of translation that belongs to preindividual forces. These forces seem to have already been traversed by an immemorial forgetfulness that makes it impossible to reduce the saying to the said and that refers to an experience for which only a collective enunciation can take responsibility. Recall the passage in which Benjamin brings out that aspect of things:

> What has been forgotten—and this insight affords us yet another avenue of access to Kafka's work—*is never something purely individual.* Everything forgotten mingles with what has been forgotten of the prehistoric world, forms countless, uncertain, changing compounds, yielding a constant flow of new, strange products. Oblivion is the container from which the *inexhaustible intermediate world* in Kafka's stories presses toward the light. (p. 131; my emphasis)

The reader of Deleuze and Guattari's book on Kafka will readily perceive that they took it upon themselves to pick up the analysis of Kafka's work where Benjamin—not because of a lack of perceptiveness but, perhaps, because of the epistemological anchoring of his text—seemed to have reached an insurmountable barrier, a dead end. Despite his efforts, Benjamin was not always able to avoid the stumbling block that he calls Kafka's "failure" and that he ultimately characterizes in terms of a shortcoming (thereby being too quick to take literally what was merely one threshold of Kafka's work):

> This document [the testament that orders the destruction of his works upon his death], which no one interested in Kafka can disregard, says that the writings did not satisfy their author, that he regarded his efforts as failures, that he counted himself among those who were bound to fail. He did fail in his grandiose attempt to convert poetry [*Dichtung*] into doctrine, to turn it into a parable and restore it to that stability and unpretentiousness which, in the face of reason, seemed to him to be the only appropriate thing for it. No other writer [*Dichter*] has obeyed the commandment "Thou shalt not make unto thee a graven image" so faithfully. (p. 129)

Without reading too much into the text, we can see a hint of nihilism that tilts Kafka's work—otherwise very positive—in the direction of the literature of failure: not far removed from Camus and his philosophy of the absurd and of the futility of every human work. Too human. But in writing *Kafka*, Deleuze and Guattari propose an experimentation of Kafka that refrains from—even in the name of a solemn *gestus*—referring to any idea of failure, of shortcoming, or of "immemorial" guilt. This book represents a watershed and is invaluable for the modern reader of Kafka: instead of seeking to capture his work in one of the "segments" that constantly draw it toward some black hole, Oedipus, or failure (in short, nihilism), Deleuze and Guattari do their utmost to resist. They successfully show that although the different diabolical machines—letters, novellas, and so-called unfinished novels—that Kafka created throughout his life do derive from a *gestus* that is constantly running the risk of annihilation, destruction, or regression, it is nonetheless wholly impossible to reduce the specific *effects* to the nihilistic figures that we have enumerated in reference to Benjamin. For Deleuze and Guattari, Kafka's work is characterized by the total absence of negation: above all, by a total absence of complacency (even in his journals) and consequently a rejection of every problematic of failure. Those who read this book carefully will perceive that the authors tried to show that Kafka's work is in no way susceptible to an anthropological or psychological explanation but is essentially the bearer of an affirmation without reserve.

Without seeming to deal with the question at all, Deleuze and Guattari begin by detaching Kafka from what the academic institution calls "Literature." It quickly becomes obvious that Kafka has been misinterpreted and, from a certain point of view, "misunderstood" only because he has for a long time—too long, according to the authors—been judged to be the embodiment of a concept of literature (and of the Law—of Genre, of Desire) that is totally inapplicable to his work. Deleuze and Guattari do not simply say that Kafka was unconcerned with literature or that he was not a writer by occupation. Instead, they break down the complex mechanism whose operation—because one is driven to "categorize" it—leads precisely to failure: an always excessive reduction of his work.

By proposing the concept of "minor literature"—a concept that opens so many new avenues of research in Europe and the United States—Deleuze and Guattari give the modern reader a means by which to enter into Kafka's work without being weighted down by the old categories of genres, types, modes, and style (in the "linguistic" sense of the term, as Barthes would say). These categories would imply that the reader's task is at bottom to *interpret* Kafka's writing, whether the interpretation take the form of parabolism, negative theology, allegory, symbolism, "correspondences," and so on. The concept of minor literature permits a reversal: instead of Kafka's work being related to some preexistent category or literary genre, it will henceforth serve as a *rallying point* or *model* for certain texts and "bi-lingual"[2] writing practices that, until now, had to pass through a long purgatory before even being read, much less recognized.

Why has it been necessary to introduce this category of minor literature to account for Kafka's work? First, because Kafka, in his *Diaries* and "theoretical" texts, meditated at length on the type of "literature" that he believed himself to be inventing and that he saw certain of his contemporaries practicing. If we reread Kafka's *Diaries* in light of what the authors bring out in this book, it immediately becomes apparent how important it was for Kafka to situate the type of writing and rewriting he was practicing. Commentators have been too quick to label as mystical (neurotic?) or metaphysical meditations that always took the form of a radical questioning of classical or traditional literary writing. Kafka does not read and admire Goethe and Flaubert to imitate them, much less to move beyond (*aufheben*) them according to some teleological schema like that of Hegel, but to determine and appreciate the incommensurable distance that separates him from their ideal of depth or perfection. Writing against the current and from a linguistic space that is radically heterogeneous with respect to his great predecessors, Kafka appears as the initiator of a new literary continent: a continent where reading and writing open up new perspectives, break ground for new avenues of thought, and, above all, wipe out the tracks of an old topography of mind and thought. With Kafka—at least with the Kafka that Deleuze and Guattari think through anew—one has the feeling that literature has been given a new face: it has changed both its addresser and its addressee.

The new category of minor literature is also essential because it allows one to dispense with dualisms and rifts—whether linguistic, generic, or even political—that have ultimately constituted a sort of vulgate (a fortress, if you will) that, although not indisputable, has been at least sufficiently restricting to impede access to what has been characterized as Kafka's "epoch": Einstein and his deterritorialization of the representation of the universe; the twelve-tone Austrians and their deterritorializations of musical representation (Marie's death cry in Wozzeck or that of Lulu); expressionist cinema and its double movement of deterritorialization and reterritorialization of the image (Robert Wiene of Czech origin, Fritz Lang born in Vienna, Paul Wegener and his use of themes from Prague); the Copernican revolution of Freud; and finally, the linguistic revolution carried out by the Prague circle. All the elements are brought together for a radical change of *épistémé* that Kafka contrives to transcribe with the most diverse means, the most complex methods. The readers of this book—if they are not in a hurry—will certainly be impressed by the extreme care that Deleuze and Guattari have taken first in describing, and then in analyzing, the variety of those methods. Whether it is a question of the relation of Kafka's texts to the German language or to the economy of writing, the authors emphasize the procedures that Kafka sets to work to produce the effect(s) that are linked to his name today: the Kafka effect.

It will come as no surprise to readers familiar with Deleuze and Guattari's work that the idea of the machine producing effects is not used metaphorically or symbolically but always in the most concrete sense. In his *Dialogues* with Claire Parnet, Deleuze makes it more precise:

> "Machine, machinism, *machinic*": it is neither mechanical nor organic. The mechanical is a system of gradual connections between dependent terms. The machine, on the other hand, is a clustered "proximity" between independent terms (topological proximity is itself independent of distance or contiguity). A machinic assemblage is defined by the displacement of a center of gravity onto an abstract line.[3]

From this perspective, we can more easily understand that there will always be a "primary" social machine in relation to human beings and animals (within the limits of what Deleuze calls its *phylum*): a gesture coming from the East will always presuppose an Asiatic machine that without preceding it in time will condition the situations in which it can be concretely effected. But in the same way that every mechanical element presupposes a social machine, the organism in turn presupposes a *body without organs* that, by means of its lines (of flight), its axes of intervention, and its "gradients," will largely exceed the ectodermal limits of the human body as well as the psychological representatives of its identity.

For Deleuze and Guattari, if Kafka still occupies the place granted him in the history of letters, it has little or nothing to do with the fact that he renewed its "themes" or transformed its style. Instead, they see him as important because he figured out a mode of writing that allows us to account for the different "machines" that condition our actual relation to the world, to the body, to desire, and to the economy of life and death. And even if he has *paredre* – brothers of blood and affection – he has no predecessor. Deleuze and Guattari are especially interested in foregrounding some of the effects produced in relating ("classical") literature and the *minority machine* in Kafka's work. It is not only a question of tapping libidinal energy but also one of opening up new registers of thought and action – of speed:

> This question of speed is important and very complicated as well. It doesn't mean to be the first to finish; one might be late by speed. Nor does it mean always changing; one might be invariable and constant by speed. Speed is to be caught in a becoming that is not a development or an evolution. One would have to be like a taxi, a waiting line, a line of flight, a bottleneck, a traffic jam, green and red lights, slight paranoia, difficult relations with the police. Being an abstract and broken line, a zigzag that slips "between." (*Dialogues*, pp. 40-41)

Thus, Kafka's work is revolutionary in the way it affects the language in which it is effected. A language that is a "major" language is affected by a strong deterritorialization factor and is subjected to a series of displacements that make it slow down to a crawl in certain texts (contexts) (see, for example, "The Metamorphosis") or send it into a panic, unfolding at a vertiginous pace (see one of the short texts, like "The Cares of a Family Man"). For Kafka, therefore, it is never a matter of "trafficking" in language or of mishandling it – how many writers and poets have supposedly "subverted" language without ever having caused the slightest ripple in comparison with the language of Kafka, Joyce, or Kleist? – but of essentially proposing a new *way of using* it. This new usage in effect short-circuits the appeal – within and by means of the "paper language" that for Kafka is German – to a higher, dominant reality (transcendent or transcendental) that would function from within as a principle of subjectivization. In Deleuzian terms, that new "language" (of a "logothete," as Barthes[4] would say) performs an "absolute deterritorialization of the cogito" by the processes that it sets to work.[5] If, according to Deleuze and Guattari, the principal strata that bind and imprison the human being are "the organism, meaningfulness, interpretation, subjectivization, and subjection" (*Mille Plateaux*, p. 167), then "minor" language is the instrument *par excellence* of that destratification.

We can now better understand what separates Benjamin's "interpretation" from the "course" taken in Deleuze and Guattari's book. What in Benjamin gives way in a (blind? asymbolic?) gesture that refers to failure here takes the path of an experimentation of life: the setting into place of a "field of continuous intensities" and of an "emission of sign-particles" that can no longer lead to failure because the security of a subject is no longer necessary. The authors show that referring Kafka's work to an idea of failure necessarily implies the full-fledged return of literary and philosophical categories that presuppose a logical, even ontological, priority of content over form: "since the content is given in a given form, one has to find, discover, or see the form of expression appropriate to it." But with Kafka it turns out that this schema and this *vection*, which seem so natural, are radically put into question.

In other words, if Kafka's watchword was really "Thou shall not make unto thee a graven image," it was certainly not in the manner of the "Turks" or "Muslims" that Hegel describes in his *Aesthetics*—those people who "forbid the painting or reproduction of the human being or any living creature"[6]—and even less like Plato—who in *The Republic* condemns art as the "greatest danger" or as simulacrum: a simulacrum that leads those who do not possess the antidotes of reason and knowledge (that is, animals, children, and the ignorant, as Kofman reminds us) to lose track of the distinction between the sophist and the philosopher, between truth and illusion.

According to the authors, it was because he liked children, animals, and the "ignorant" that Kafka understood how to effect the strongest challenge to the wall of censure erected by the history of literature. Like the animal that could never really have a thought because it would simultaneously forget what it was on the verge of thinking (a process Nietzsche discussed in his *Untimely Meditations*), "minor" literature as reinvented by Kafka "begins by expressing itself and doesn't conceptualize until afterward" (p. 28). With Kafka we are no longer confronted by a "dialectic" or a "structural" correspondence between two kinds of "forms"—forms of content, on the one hand, and ready-made forms of expression, on the other—but, in the authors' words, by a *machine of expression* that is capable of disorganizing its own forms, of disorganizing the forms of content, so as to free up an intense material of expression that is then made of pure content that can no longer be separated from its expression:

> Expression must break forms, encourage ruptures and new sproutings. When a form is broken, one must reconstruct the content that will necessarily be part of a rupture in the order of things. To take over, to anticipate, the material. (p. 28)

Thus, the art (*modern* art in this sense) that Kafka tried to introduce is effectively no longer an art that proposes to "express" (a meaning), to "represent" (a thing, a being), or to "imitate" (a nature). It is rather a method (of writing)—of picking up, even of stealing: of "double stealing" as Deleuze sometimes says, which is both "stealing" and "stealing away"—that consists in propelling the most diverse contents on the basis of (nonsignifying) ruptures and intertwinings of the most heterogeneous orders of signs and powers. The familial triangle, for example, is connected to other triangles (such as commercial, economic, bureaucratic, and juridical ones), and thus the "individual concern" finds itself linked directly to the political. According to Deleuze and Guattari, the second principal characteristic of minor literature is that it is always political, not only in the sense in which one speaks of politics, but specifically in the sense in which further activity is no longer related to a unified instance, to an autonomous subjective substance that would be the *origin* of the choices we make, of the tastes we have, and of the life we lead.

In that sense, each and every gesture takes on a quasi-cosmic dimension. Benjamin says it well:

> Kafka does not grow tired of representing the *gestus* in this fashion, but he invariably does so with astonishment. . . . Experiments have proved that a man does not recognize his own walk on the screen or his own voice on the phonograph. The situation of the subject in such experiments is Kafka's situation; this is what directs him to learning, where he may encounter fragments of his own existence, fragments that are still within the context of the role. (p. 137)

But it is with regard to the apparently "fragmentary" character of Kafkaesque exegeses that Deleuze and Guattari once again differ from Benjamin. Although Benjamin never tried to relate Kafka's work to a previous text or record that would allow one to "explain" it, his text does remain tacitly saturated with considerations that refer more or less directly to Jewish theology. Did Benjamin not write to Scholem in 1939 that "anybody who could see the comic sides of Jewish theology would at the same time have in hand the *key* to Kafka"?[7]

In fact, at the end of his dense study of Kafka, when it is a matter of accounting for the "law" of the work and bringing to light the internal principle that Kafka himself followed, Benjamin refers to the loss of the Holy Writ. Kafka's work somehow remains enigmatic, his life and attitude incomprehensible and mysterious: "Kafka, however, has found the law of his journey—at least on one occasion he succeeded in bringing its breathtaking speed in line with the slow narrative pace that he presumably sought all his life" (p. 139).

Seen from a certain angle, Deleuze and Guattari's book on Kafka represents the annulment of such a question because—as they do their best to show—if there is one thing that should be avoided besides the natural (psychoanalytic) explanation and the supernatural (theological) one, it is the temptation to draw Kafka toward the "individual concern," the tragic (that is, toward personal psychology, neurosis, or an author's individual tastes). Neither allegory, metaphor, nor theology will sum up a work that has explored them all without letting itself be taken over by any single one. But, above all, neither the transcendence of the law, the internalization of guilt, nor the subjectivity of the enunciation can ever give an adequate account of the intrinsic force of Kafka's work.

Far from relating this work to an interior drama, an intimate tribunal, or something else drawn from the same old grab bag, Deleuze and Guattari ask us to be attentive to the labor of the "dismantling" or demolition of forms and categories that determine the "great literature" in Kafka. A calm dismantling—one would be tempted to say "pacific"—that first takes the form of an "a priori elimination of every idea of guilt": there are certainly many "guilty" characters in Kafka, and with an extremely strong and deleterious guilt, but Kafka never takes that guilt for granted. On the contrary, it appears at each moment as the effect of an assemblage, of a machine if you will, that indirectly takes up lawyers, judges, *and* the victims in the same movement. As Deleuze and Guattari write: "Culpability is never anything but the superficial movement whereby judges and even lawyers confine you in order to prevent you from engaging in a real movement—that is, from taking care of your own affairs" (p. 45). So much for culpability.

The dismantling mentioned above has a second aspect, and this one is decisive in confronting the reading proposed by Deleuze and Guattari with that of Benjamin: "even if the law remains unrecognizable, this is not because it is hidden by its transcendence, but simply because it is always denuded of any interiority: it is always in the office next door, or behind the door, on to infinity" (p. 45). It is very easy to see the implications that such a hypothesis entails in regard to theology (whether Jewish or another). The law is not stated in accord with its ("sham") transcendence, but the opposite occurs: "it is the statement, the enunciation, that constructs the law in the name of an immanent power of the one who enounces it—the law is confused with that which the guardian utters, and the writings precede the law, rather than being the necessary and derived expression of it" (p. 45). Transcendence of the law, the interiority of guilt, and the subjectivity of enunciation are the three "themes" that, according to Deleuze and Guattari, have misled readers and made access to Kafka's work difficult if not impossible, for it becomes inevitably a matter of relating the complexity to his "genius," to the "mystery" of his existence, as in the relationship of the Haggadah to the Halaka, which Benjamin mentions in his text on Kafka.[8] In delving into the "methods" and the processes that Kafka uses to revoke the law's mystery and relate it to the places of its enunciation, and in describing them with precision, Deleuze and Guattari make way for—perhaps for the first time—a "joyous" reading of Kafka: a *Gaya Scienza* of Kafka's work.

Free of the "three most tiresome themes" of the interpretation of the law, Deleuze and Guattari are led to propose a conception of the relation of law to desire that allows them to call into question all the ambiguities and semiobscurities that weigh down all the commentaries on Kafka's work. For them, since the law that is constantly referred to in Kafka no longer lends itself to an anthropological or theological explanation, the entire economy of that strange "work," and in particular its relation to desire (of writing, reading, and loving), has to be reinterpreted. And not only has the nature of the law been "misinterpreted," but the status and role of desire in Kafka's work have not fared any better. Deleuze and Guattari are the first to underscore the importance and force of desire in Kafka. As they reveal, this desire cannot be placed in a relation (of dependence) with a lack or even with the law in general, with a localized natural reality (the substantial "object" of my desire), or with worldly pleasure (above all the "carnivalesque"). As Deleuze and Guattari say in an essential passage in this book: *"where one believed there was the law, there is in fact desire and desire alone*. Justice is desire and not law" (p. 49).

One can guess the consequences they will draw from such premises: since desire is the effective "operator" of an assemblage where everybody – officials, judges, lawyers, artists, men, women, and so forth – is held, it becomes obvious why neither a lack nor a privation (of a transcendent meaning, for example) *gives* or causes desire; on the contrary, one can *lack* something only in relation to an assemblage from which one is excluded, but one *desires* only as a function of an assemblage where one is included: if only, as Deleuze says, in an "association of banditry or revolt" (*Dialogues*, p. 25).

Thus, we can better understand what was lacking in Benjamin's attempt to reach an interpretation by means of gesture or the Talmud: by making law into a substance and desire (for justice) into an exigency that, if not transcendent, is external to the assemblage where every subject is only one piece of a complex montage, he has to hypostatize a nature of justice and of the law. He also has to derive desire from a lack or a law that transcends the subject or, if you will, from a law that the subject has "forgotten" and that is waiting to reemerge into the light.[9] According to Deleuze and Guattari, conversely, if justice doesn't lend itself to representation, it is not because justice is inaccessible or mysteriously hidden, but because it is desire:

> Desire could never be on a stage where it would sometimes appear like a party opposed to another party (desire against the law), sometimes like the presence of the two sides under the effect of a superior law that would govern their distribution and their combination. (p. 50)

Thus, the following conclusion is drawn:

> If everything, everyone, is part of justice, if everyone is an auxiliary of justice, from the priest to the little girls, this is not because of the transcendence of the law but because of the immanence of desire. (p.50)

This last version – very Kafkaesque – of the avatars and metamorphoses of desire reveals that for Kafka there is never any need for a representative to intercede between him and his desire, just as there is no need for an intermediary between the "work" of the text and the reader. Because it is *immanent*, the desire that traverses Kafka's work doesn't even require what Benjamin, in referring to Father Malebranche (!), claims for Kafka himself: for instance, the possession of *attentiveness*, "the natural prayer of the soul." On the contrary, Kafka knew that to find justice—the justice that he was seeking, that traversed him—it was necessary to move, to go from one room to another, from office to office, from language to language, and from country to country, always following his desire.

To find the "key" to Kafka's work, Deleuze and Guattari haven't sought to interpret it; they didn't seek to relate it to some single, transcendent law. Like K., the man of the immanent quest following the line of infinite flight, they have tried to grapple with the extraordinary machine of expression that Kafka set to work and have taken up the task of rewriting the quest to infinity, interminably. In reading this short but very dense book, we find, in place of infinite *exegesis*, a reading of Kafka's work that is *practical*: "continuum of desire, with shifting limits that are always displaced" (p. 51). It is this procedure in action, this continuous process, and this field of immanence that Deleuze and Guattari have tried to help us traverse with a Kafka freed from his interpreters.

# Translator's Introduction

> Reading a text is never a scholarly exercise in search of what is
> signified, still less a highly textual exercise in search of a signifer.
> Rather, it is a productive use of the literary machine, a montage
> of desiring machines, a schizoid exercise that extracts from the
> text its revolutionary force.
> —Deleuze and Guattari, *Anti-Oedipus*

How to translate *Kafka* by Deleuze and Guattari? Perhaps one way to answer
this necessary question would be to make a detour through another question, the
apparent simplicity of which actually connects to a whole complex panoply of
questions about the functions and uses of critical theory today, about the ties of
literary analysis and philosophical investigation, about the very status of writing
in contemporary thought and practice. This second question: why translate
*Kafka*?

Against the ease of a Sir Edmund Hillary sort of answer—"Because it's
there"—I want to suggest that to construct an effective translation of the text, we
need to reflect on the role(s) of *Kafka*, of the energy it can possess for readers
in varying situations, in varying emplacements and inscriptions within the fields
of knowledge today. For the question of translation is also a question of politics
and audience: for whom should this book be translated, and to what end?

Immediately, then, a first answer: *Kafka* is not a book designed for the usual
purposes of what we might term the Kafka-specialist—or at least not for that specialist insofar as he or she remains a specialist, a disciplinary force who reter-

ritorializes the openness of a writing (in this case Kafka's) onto the facts of a life, the teleology of a biography frequently studied in itself and cut off from all exteriorities. Indeed, there seems at first glance to be little here that could interest the scholar-specialist, that could add new information to his or her pool of authorial knowledge. To be sure, Deleuze and Guattari's evident debt to an existential phenomenology in which style is understood to be an energetic and total investment of an author's (political) being-in-the-world means that *Kafka* can bear a certain resemblance to the traditional study of an author as some kind of necessary and transparent linking up of life and art in a univocally causal fashion.

But *Kafka* is not a book of life explaining art, or vice versa. To be sure, there is a certain teleology as Deleuze and Guattari narrate a turn in Kafka from short story to novel as an attempt to resolve certain problems. But contrary to, say, Sartre, who in *L'Idiot de la famille* presents the literary developments in a biography as a supreme solution *to the psychological problems of a life* (in this case Flaubert's hang-ups with Dad), Deleuze and Guattari don't see writing as a solution to the interiorized problems of an individual psychology. Rather, writing stands against psychology, against interiority, by giving an author a possibility of becoming more than his or her nominal self, of trading the insistent solidity of the family tree for the whole field of desire and history. The romance of the individual life is exceeded, deterritorialized, escaped. Only in this sense is *Kafka* "about" Kafka.

At the extreme, the book may even seem a failure in the eyes of the traditional literary critic's defense of the organic integrity, coherence, and complexity of the authorial career; hence, the dismissive review by Guy Scarpetta in, of all places, *Tel Quel*—a journal one might have assumed to have little need for investment in old(er) mythologies of the author, although the journal's recent reincarnation as a born-again Christian journal might suggest retrospectively the extent to which the journal was always already tied to an ideology of the Author and His Word. For Scarpetta, *Kafka*'s "failure" (the term is his) comes from its reduction of a whole career to a single philosophic force—from its desire to "present texts as 'examples' (if not as 'symptoms') instead of analyzing the process they engage in" (Scarpetta 1975, 49).

Precisely. Except for his attribution to Deleuze and Guattari of the term *symptom*, which they would probably disavow as being too indebted to an ideology of interpretation, as a dive into the hermeneutic depths, Scarpetta (no matter how critically) seems to capture something of the Deleuze-Guattari project, of their particular stance toward the individual author. We might say that for them, *Kafka* is really a pretext, no more, or less, than one of the many ways to enter into the field of history, to find oneself (or one's many selves, to refer to the way that Deleuze and Guattari describe their collaboration at the beginning of *Milles Plateaux*) carried away on one of history's many, many lines of escape.

Indeed, the layering, connective, montagist entity called *Milles Plateaux* already seems to be germinating in *Kafka*, where the discussion of the nominal subject always seems to be taking place in conjunction with—or as Deleuze and Guattari might say, in adjacency with—a whole array of other subjects: Sacher-Masoch, Orson Welles, Marcel Proust, Samuel Beckett, and James Joyce, to name just a few.

To be sure, it is not the case that the book is not about Kafka, and it demonstrates a certain concern for that kind of comprehensiveness of research that traditional criticism demands in the study of a life; Deleuze and Guattari have gone through the full range of the primary texts and have covered the essential secondary literature. Their reading of Kafka seems to stand as a challenge to previous readings of Kafka—especially to that present reading of Kafka as a misanthrope of negativity, a case of Oedipalized neurosis, a refugee into the interiority of subjectivity as against the collective enunciation of mass political action. And, no doubt, the Deleuze-Guattari reading of Kafka as man of joy, as promoter of a radical politics, as rejecter of all submissions to the ostensible ties of family and neurosis could no doubt become part of the canon of the Kafka discipline.

However, throughout *Kafka*, Deleuze and Guattari argue that such a reading goes beyond specializations and disciplinary boundaries. Indeed, by treating previous readings of Kafka as forms of reterritorialization of a nomadic writing, Deleuze and Guattari suggest how the seeming integrity of academic specialization is actually an alibi for an inevitable exploitation of literary criticism to political ends. Thus, although Deleuze and Guattari's reading of bent head–straightened head images as processes of submission and defiance, as against Marthe Robert's reading of such images as signifiers of "impossible quests," can seem like the sort of interpretative quibble from within that so often characterizes literary criticism, one of the longest footnotes of *Kafka*, on the changing history of communist attitudes toward Kafka, emphasizes how all readings—including by retrospective implication Marthe Robert's seemingly innocent one—are political practices that can contain and constrain, impel and empower. In the cartography of desire and history, the smallest quibble immediately opens onto the whole map of political struggle in all its complex dimensions. Not that literary criticism is in any way a metaphor for larger struggles; rather, it is a place of such struggles. Notions of larger and smaller become inappropriate and come to be replaced by the possibility of a micropolitics where everything is immediately and necessarily contiguous with everything else.

It is as if the book before us is only one version, one twist of the kaleidoscope (to use an image from Guattari), of an infinitely permutating, connecting process in which the single event—here, the life of Kafka—is never more than one step in a larger process. Some of the other versions seem bracketed out by the provisional or initial centering of this book on Kafka—indeed, the discussion of

Sacher-Masoch literally takes place inside a set of parentheses that typographi-
cally set it off from the rest of the book—but *Kafka* still seems specifically nomadic, its own writing echoing that opening up, which Deleuze and Guattari im-
pute to Kafka, of any single event to the whole force of history. Kafka becomes
an example, one case within a typology of cases. Even in a book that bears his
name, Kafka has no more, or less, ultimate privilege than any other subject. (We
might compare this to the strategic process of Deleuze's *L'Image-Mouvement* in
which the "très belle oeuvre" of horror director Mario Bava has an equal standing with the work of Bergman or Bergson.) In this sense, *Kafka* participates in
that process of equalization of human phenomena implicit in the semiotic enterprise undertaken by Deleuze and Guattari, an enterprise that Deleuze suggests
has as its role to "be nothing more than a study of regimes, of their differences,
and their transformations" (Deleuze 1977, 127).

Franz Kafka, Sigmund Freud, David Hume, Francis Bacon, Sam Fuller, and
so on—whatever the particular subject at any particular moment of Deleuze and
Guattari's semiotic, whether this subject is still locked into older ideologies of
lack, of repression (as Deleuze and Guattari argue is the case with Freud, Lacan,
and their followers) or whether the subject is, in Edward Said's term, between
system and culture and so able to anticipate the political currents of the future
(as Deleuze and Guattari argue is the case with the nomads like Kafka, Beckett,
and Nicholas Ray)—in all cases, the figures share in desire, in expression, in
the razor's edge confrontation of territorialization, deterritorialization, and reterritorialization. Semiotic equalization, then, doesn't mean indiscrimination, an
anarchic or existentialist acceptance of all practices as a justifiable assumption
of one's own freedom. Deleuze and Guattari obviously do evaluate, do believe
that certain practices stand a better chance of opening up to multiplicity. They
prefer their Kafka to Marthe Robert's; as Deleuze explains, the goal of their
reading process is to "bring to an author a little of this joy, this amorous political
life that he knew how to offer, how to invent. So many dead writers must have
wept over what was written about them. I hope that Kafka enjoyed the book that
we wrote about him" (Deleuze 1977, 142).

In a sense, if the biographical Kafka hadn't existed, Deleuze and Guattari
could have invented him or found another version of his semiotic elsewhere.
Thus, one doesn't translate for the specialist. One translates for the deterritorializing critic who, to use a term that Deleuze uses to describe his and Guattari's
procedure, engages in a "pickup" of ideas (Deleuze 1977), a gathering here and
there of desires, of wills, of energies. The translation aims to continue that picking up of *Kafka* for all sorts of purposes other than the study of Kafka in particular. Among the recent work inspired by *Kafka*, I would cite *"A White Heron"
and the Question of Minor Literature*, Louis Renza's study of the minority position in American letters of the provincial, female writer (Renza 1984), and Réda
Bensmaïa's *"Amour bilingue* de Khatibi," a commentary on the dialogic practice

of a Maghrebian writing that may undo French from within (Bensmaïa 1985). These writings use Deleuze and Guattari's book to theorize all sorts of differential practices of writing and to suggest how placing any minority writer within a major language can turn into a battle of the most far-reaching sort.

Not that one should applaud any use of *Kafka* whatsoever. Already, some of the American critical adulation of other Deleuze-Guattari texts, especially *Anti-Oedipus*, suggests how quickly a politics of the rhizomatic can assuage the unhappy guilty conscience of the depoliticized intellectual by offering him or her the alibi of a process in which everything one does can be something that one can pretend is politically engaged. The notion of the rhizome as an endless pattern in which everything is linked to everything else can lead to a slide from a notion like the Leninist one of struggle as a calculated engagement with the *weakest* link in the chain to a kind of anarcho-voluntarist fantasy that every link is, in every place and time, equally weak, equally appropriate as a point of application for one's critical energies. Dangerously, despite all the efforts of Deleuze and Guattari to deconstruct hierarchies, American literary criticism may treat them the way it has generally treated Mikhail Bakhtin (in many ways a very similar sort of thinker)—not as theorists of the ties of collective enunciation and minor literature but as aesthetes of a high-culture avant-garde closed in on its own fetishes of interiority. Deleuze and Guattari themselves admit that there is a fine line between territorializing and deterritorializing processes, and it is easy for their work to be appropriated to the most divergent and even contradictory of ends. One hopes that a translation of *Kafka* will be something that readers will question, as well as use.

It is necessary to keep watch over the ways in which what Deleuze and Guattari present as progressive deterritorializations may necessitate simultaneous reterritorializations in other sites of the rhizome. Most especially, as Alice Jardine has pointed out, the lines of escape tend to be especially open to privileged male figures; for all their talk of a *devenir-femme*, a becoming–woman, Deleuze and Guattari tend to abstract this process away from any tie to the historically specific situation and struggle of women. Men get a chance to take flight from their entrapment, but women get no chance at all except to be perfectly invisible in the flow of the discourse (Jardine 1985). A picking up of Deleuze and Guattari, then, would have to examine not only what they enable but also what they disenable, what they close off. Deleuze and Guattari's throwaway references to Kafka's schizo-incest with the sister may well promote the male writer's rejection of an Oedipal triangulation for the sake of a certain polymorphous perversity, but they can also elide the sister's place in all of this: to what extent might not Franz's (or Deleuze and Guattari's) need for a deterritorialization of the Kafka-machine require a certain reterritorialization of the sister—her reification into a myth of Femininity as a kind of succoring aid to the adventuring male in his quest to go beyond limits?

This means that *Kafka* shouldn't stand as a static collection of polished, finished ideas or mythologies or ideologies that one would pick up for their precision and ready-made profundity. If *Kafka* escapes from allegiance to a Kafka-life, the depths of a romance of Kafka the man, this escape should not lead to the assumption that one can ever fully escape *to* something else, to a final point at the end of a line. In a sense, *Kafka* can do what Deleuze and Guattari say that Kafka was doing; each moment in the writing is only a sort of room that one can leave by going through a door, only to arrive in another room that one won't stay in and that has doors that, in turn, lead to other rooms. Hence, I attempt in this translation to reiterate (I avoid saying "reproduce," a word too tied to a mimesis) a flow of Deleuze and Guattari's text. Even though it is possible throughout the text for a reader to believe that he or she catches the real and full sense beneath the frequently allusive, elusive movement of the arguments, the translation doesn't attempt in any way to fill out the book, to help the multiplicities of things left unsaid take on the form of emphatic, authoritative statements.

Even the key words of the Deleuze-Guattari procedure, words like *rhizome*, *lines of escape*, *assemblage* (*agencement*), become battle-sites for a process of deterritorialization as the authors violate their own proprietary authorship of terms and make the words tremble, stutter. For example, while Deleuze and Guattari initially seem to be getting at something systematic, that is, fixed and rationalized, in a distinction between *procès* (which we might want to translate not only as "process" but also as "trial," as in the French title for Kafka's *The Trial*, a kind of processing) and *processus* (which we might be able to translate as "procedure"), the boundaries between the two give way. Seeming to refer to fixed conceptual fields, the words seem initially territorialized, literally the guardians of two inviolate and irrevocably distinct conceptual realms. But a kind of sliding contagion occurs, and through the course of the book, each term comes to refer to elements within the original territorial space of the other term. So, to a large extent, the translation lets the words slide—*procès* and *processus* interpenetrate, each engaging in unsystematic war-marchine attacks on the other.

Again, as part of the nonspecialist quality of the book, the language of *Kafka* is a language that glides between a number of accepted discourses, and it is again as an answer to the questions of translation that this translation works to convey a sense of the fields from which Deleuze and Guattari draw some of their terminology. Most important, the attempt to redefine the nature of the author leads Deleuze and Guattari to foray into the recent work in linguistics inspired by Emile Benveniste on the conditions of linguistic enunciation. Benveniste's distinction between the denoted message in a text (its enounced content) and the message that every text gives about the conditions under which it was enounced serves Deleuze and Guattari in their attempt to show how the politics of a Kafka-writing lie not only in what he says, or even in how what he says reveals a psychology of the author, but in the effects that the writing establishes in being written—in, for example, locking into the historical currents that are knocking at the door of the lone author's study. The English reader should know then that the discussions of enunciation here take part in a larger French discussion of significance as residing as much in the performative aspects of language as in its referential ones. (See, for example, the entire issue of the important semiotics journal *Communications* that is devoted to the question of "Cinema and Enunciation" [1983].) In line with the forthcoming translation of *Milles Plateaux*, I have translated Benveniste's terms as "enunciation" (*énonciation*) and as "statement" (*énoncé*), although readers should keep in mind the ambiguities of this latter translation choice in comparison with Benveniste's essentially and deliberately univocal term, the *énoncé* being precisely that myth of a fixed, dictionarylike content to a message.

In only one way, perhaps, have I made use of the Kafka discipline; most of the translations of the citations from Kafka come from the standard Muir translations. Although Joyce Crick suggests that the Muirs tended to translate Kafka as a writer of bleak negativity (Crick 1980), and although the French translation seems to express more of that virtually carnivalesque joy that Deleuze and Guattari read in Kafka, it seemed to me that the inscription of the Muir version within the Deleuze-Guattari text might already encourage that kind of active escaping that Deleuze and Guattari work to establish for Kafka. That is, the presence of a territorializing voice—the Muir's version of Kafka as an insistently misanthropic, isolated poor soul—increases the gamble of Deleuze and Guattari's project. Like the emphatic reductiveness of the French Communist party's (in)famous "Faut-il brûler Kafka?" ("Should we burn Kafka?"), the bleak univocality of the Muir version of Kafka increases the intensity of the struggle and shows how much is at stake in Deleuze and Guattari's attempt to constitute literary criticism as one of the most advanced branches of the Joyful Science.

I wish to thank the following people for assistance in the preparation of this manuscript: Professor Clark Muenzer of the University of Pittsburgh for bibliographic and citational information on some of the texts by and on Kafka; and Drs. Pradheep Sindhu and Marie-Françoise Bertrand of Palo Alto for computer assistance and support.

D.P.

## BIBLIOGRAPHY

Bensmaïa, Réda. "Traduire ou 'blanchir' la langue: *Amour Bilingue* d'Abdelkebir Khatibi." *Hors Cadre* 3 (Spring 1985):187–206.

*Communications* 38: *Cinema et enonciation* (1983).

Crick, Joyce. "Kafka and the Muirs." In *The World of Franz Kafka*, edited by J. P. Stern, 159–97. New York: Holt, Rinehart and Winston, 1980.

Deleuze, Gilles, and Claire Parnet, *Dialogues.* Paris: Flammarion, 1977

Jardine, Alice. "Deleuze and His Br(others)." *Sub-Stance* 13, No. 3–4 (1984):46–60.

Renza, Louis. *"A White Heron" and the Question of Minor Literature.* Milwaukee: University of Wisconsin Press, 1984.

Scarpetta, Guy. Review of *Kafka*, by Deleuze and Guattari. *Tel Quel* 63 (Autumn 1975):48–49.

# Kafka: Toward a Minor Literature

# Chapter 1
# Content and Expression

How can we enter into Kafka's work? This work is a rhizome, a burrow. The castle has multiple entrances whose rules of usage and whose locations aren't very well known. The hotel in *Amerika* has innumerable main doors and side doors that innumerable guards watch over; it even has entrances and exits without doors. Yet it might seem that the burrow in the story of that name has only one entrance; the most the animal can do is dream of a second entrance that would serve only for surveillance. But this is a trap arranged by the animal and by Kafka himself; the whole description of the burrow functions to trick the enemy. We will enter, then, by any point whatsoever; none matters more than another, and no entrance is more privileged even if it seems an impasse, a tight passage, a siphon. We will be trying only to discover what other points our entrance connects to, what crossroads and galleries one passes through to link two points, what the map of the rhizome is and how the map is modifed if one enters by another point. Only the principle of multiple entrances prevents the introduction of the enemy, the Signifier and those attempts to interpret a work that is actually only open to experimentation.

We'll start with a modest way in—that of *The Castle*'s inn parlor where K discovers the *portrait* of a porter with his *head bent*, his chin sunk into his chest. These two elements—the portrait or the photo, and the beaten and bent head— are constant in Kafka, although there are varying degrees of autonomy of one from the other. The photo of the parents in *Amerika*. The portrait of the woman in fur in "The Metamorphosis" (there an actual mother has a bent head, and an actual father wears a porter's uniform). Proliferation of photos and portraits in

3

*The Trial* from Fraulein Burstner's room to Titorelli's studio. The bent head that one can no longer raise appears all the time in the letters, in the Notebooks, in the Diaries, in the stories, and also in *The Trial* where the judges have their backs bent against the ceiling, against some of the assistants, the executioner, the priest and so on. Thus, the entrance we have chosen not only promises to connect with things that we hope will eventually appear in the work but is itself constituted by the connecting of two relatively independent forms, the form of content (the bent head) and the form of expression (portrait-photo), which re-unite at the beginning of *The Castle*. We aren't interpreting them. We would simply say that this reunion causes a functional blockage, a neutralization of ex-perimental desire—the untouchable, unkissable, forbidden, enframed photo that can only take pleasure (*jouir*) from its own sight, like that desire blocked by the roof or the ceiling, a submissive desire that can only take pleasure from its own submission. And also the desire that imposes submission, propagates it; a desire that judges and condemns (like the father in "The Judgment" who so bends his head that his son has to kneel before him). Memory of an Oedipal childhood? The memory is a family portrait or a vacation photo showing men with bent heads, women with their necks circled by a ribbon.[1] The memory blocks desire, makes mere carbon copies of it, fixes it within strata, cuts it off from all its con-nections. But what, then, can we hope for? It's an impasse. Nonetheless, we can realize that even an impasse is good if it forms part of the rhizome.

The head that straightens, the head that bursts through the roof or the ceiling, seems an answer to the bent head. We find it everywhere in Kafka.[2] In *The Cas-tle*, the portrait of the porter is matched by the evocation of the hometown church steeple that "*firm in line, soar[ed] unfalteringly* to its tapering point" (even the tower of the castle, as a machine of desire, evokes the melancholy, mad movement of an inhabitant who would have risen by breaking through the roof). Yet isn't the image of the small-town steeple still a memory? Actually, it no longer acts as such. Rather, it acts as a childhood block, and not as a child-hood memory, strengthening desire instead of cramping it, displacing it in time, deterritorializing it, proliferating its connections, linking it to other intensities (thus, as a block, the tower-steeple connects to two other scenes, that of the teacher and of the children whose words are incomprehensible, and that of the displaced, redressed, or reversed family scene in which it is the adults who play around in the tub). But that's not important. What's important is the light music, or, more precisely, the pure and intense sound emanating from the steeple and the castle tower: "a bell began to ring merrily up there, a bell that for at least a second made his heart palpitate for its tone was menacing, too, as if it threat-ened him with the fulfillment of his vague desire. This great bell soon died away, however, and its place was taken by a feeble, monotonous little twinkle." It's cu-rious how the intrusion of sound often occurs in Kafka in connection with the movement to raise or straighten the head—Josephine the mouse, the young musical dogs ("Everything was music, the lifting and setting down of their feet. . . . the symmetrical patterns which they produced by one dog setting his front paws on the back of another and the rest following suit . . . They were walking on their hind legs."). The distinction between two states of desire appears especially in "The Metamorphosis" when, on the one hand, Gregor glues himself to the *portrait* of the woman in fur and bends his head toward the door in a desperate attempt to hold onto something in his room (which is being emptied out), and when, on the other hand, Gregor leaves this room, guided by the vibrating *sound* of the violin, and tries to grab onto the uncovered neck of his sister (who has stopped wearing collars or ribbons ever since she lost her social standing). Is this the difference between a plastic and still Oedipal incest with a maternal photo and a schizo incest with the sister and the light music that emerges strangely from it? Music always seems caught up in an indivisible becoming-child or becoming-animal, a sonorous block that opposes the visual memory. "Please turn out the light, I can only play in the dark. *I straightened myself.*"[3] We could well believe that these are two new forms: the straightened head is a form of content, and the musical sound is a form of expression. Shall we represent all this through the following equations?

$$\frac{\text{bent head}}{\text{portrait-photo}} = \text{a blocked, oppressed or oppressing, neutralized desire, with a minimum of connection, childhood memory, territoriality or reterritorialization.}$$

$$\frac{\text{straightened head}}{\text{musical sound}} = \text{a desire that straightens up or moves forward, and opens up to new connections, childhood block or animal block, deterritorialization.}$$

But that's not really right. It is certainly not a systematized music, a musical form, that interests Kafka (in his letters and in his diary, one finds nothing more than insignificant anecdotes about a few musicians). It isn't a composed and semiotically shaped music that interests Kafka, but rather a pure sonorous material. If one counts the main scenes of sonorous intrusions, one arrives approximately at the following list: the John Cage–like concert in *Description of a Struggle* where the supplicant (1) wants to play the piano because he is feeling happy; (2) doesn't know how to play; (3) doesn't play at all ("At that moment two gentlemen seized the bench and, whistling a song and rocking me to and fro, carried me far away from the piano to the dining table"); and (4) is congratulated for having played so well. In the "Investigations of a Dog," the musical dogs produce a tremendous racket, but no one can tell how they do it, since they don't speak, sing, or bark but make the music swell up out of nothingness. In "Josephine the Singer, or the Mouse Folk," it is unlikely that Josephine really sings; she only whistles in a way that is no better than any other mouse, perhaps even worse, but in such a manner that the mystery of her nonexistent art becomes even greater. In *Amerika*, Karl Rossman plays too quickly or too slowly, ridiculously, and feels "rising within him a song which reach[es] past the end of this song." In "The Metamorphosis," sound intervenes at first as a faint whining that captures Gregor's voice and blurs the resonance of words; and then, even though she's a musician, the sister manages to do no more than pluck at her violin, bothered by the shadow of the boarders.

These examples sufficiently show that in the realm of expression, sound is not opposed to the portait, *as* the straightened head was opposed to the bent head in the realm of content. If we consider the two forms of content abstractly, there is undeniably a simple formal opposition between them, a binary relation, a structural or semantic quality that scarcely lets us out of the realm of the signifier and that is more a dichotomy than a rhizome. But whereas the portait, for its part, is undeniably a form of expression that corresponds to a form of the content "bent head," this is not so for sound. What interests Kafka is a pure and intense sonorous material that is always connected to *its own abolition* — a deterritorialized musical sound, a cry that escapes signification, composition, song, words — a sonority that ruptures in order to break away from a chain that is still all too signifying. In sound, intensity alone matters, and such sound is generally monotone and always nonsignifying; thus, in *The Trial*, the monotone cry of a warder who is being punished "did not seem to come from a human being but from some martyred instrument."[4] As long as there is form, there is still reterritorialization, even in music. In contrast, all of Josepine's art consists in the fact that, not knowing more than the other mice how to sing, she perhaps enacts a deterritorialization of "the usual piping" and liberates it from "the cares of daily life." In short, sound doesn't show up here as a form of expression, but rather as an *unformed material of expression*, that will act on the other terms. On the one hand, it serves to express contents that will reveal themselves to be relatively less and less formalized; thus, the head that straightens up ceases to matter in itself and becomes formally no more than a deformable substance swept away by the flow of sonorous expression. As Kafka has the ape in "A Report to an Academy" say, it isn't a question of a well-formed vertical movement toward the sky or in front of one's self, it is no longer a question of breaking through the roof, but of intensely going *"head over heels and away,"* no matter where, even without moving; it isn't a question of liberty as against submission, but only a question of a line of escape or, rather, of a simple *way out*, "right, left or in any direction," as long as it is as little signifying as possible. On the other hand, the firmest and most resistant formalizations — for example, those on the order of the portrait or the bent head — will themselves lose their rigidity in order to proliferate or prepare an upheaval in which they fall into new lines of intensity (even the curved backs of the judges emit a sonorous cracking that pushes the issue of Justice out of the picture; and photos and pictures proliferate in *The Trial* to take on a new function). Kafka's drawings, the old men and the silhouettes that he liked to draw, emphasize figures with bent heads, straightened heads, and head over heels and away. Take a look at the reproductions in the Kafka issue of *Obliques*.

We won't try to find archetypes that would represent Kafka's imaginary, his dynamic, or his bestiary (the archetype works by assimilation, homogenization, and thematics, whereas our method works only where a rupturing and hetereogenous line appears). Moreover, we aren't looking for any so-called free associations (we are all well aware of the sad fate of these associations that always bring us back to childhood memories or, even worse, to the phantasm, not because they fail to work but because such a fate is part of their actual underlying principle). We aren't even trying to interpret, to say that this means that.[5] And we are looking least of all for a structure with formal oppositions and a fully constructed Signifier; one can always come up with binary oppositions like "bent head–straightened head" or "portrait-sonority" and bi-univocal relations like "bent head–portrait" or "straightened head–sonority." But that's stupid as long as one doesn't see where the system is coming from and going to, how it becomes, and what element is going to play the role of heterogeneity, a saturating body that makes the whole assembly flow away and that breaks the symbolic structure, no less than it breaks hermeneutic interpretation, the ordinary association of ideas, and the imaginary archetype. Because we don't see much difference among all these things (who could tell what the difference is between a structural, differential opposition and an imaginary archetype whose role is to differentiate itself?). We believe only in a Kafka *politics* that is neither imaginary nor symbolic. We believe only in one or more Kafka *machines* that are neither structure nor phantasm. We believe only in a Kafka *experimentation* that is without interpretation or significance and rests only on tests of experience: "I am not appealing for any man's verdict, I am only imparting knowledge, I am only making a report. To you also, honored Members of the Academy, I have only made a report."[6] A writer isn't a writer-man; he is a machine-man, and an experimental man (who thereby ceases to be a man in order to become an ape or a beetle, or a dog, or mouse, a becoming-animal, a becoming-inhuman, since it is actually through voice and through sound and through a style that one becomes an animal, and certainly through the force of sobriety).

A Kafka-machine is thus constituted by contents and expressions that have been formalized to diverse degrees by unformed materials that enter into it, and leave by passing through all possible states. To enter or leave the machine, to be in the machine, to walk around it, to approach it — these are all still components of the machine itself: these are states of desire, free of all interpretation. The line of escape is part of the machine. Inside or outside, the animal is part of the burrow-machine. The problem is not that of being free but of finding a way out, or even a way in, another side, a hallway, an adjacency. Maybe there are several factors that we must take into account: the purely superficial unity of the machine, the way in which men are themselves pieces of the machine, the position of desire (man or animal) in relation to the machine. In the "Penal Colony," the machine seems to have a strong degree of unity and the man enters completely into it. Maybe this is what leads to the final explosion and the crumbling of the machine. In *Amerika*, in contrast, K remains exterior to a whole series of machines, going from one to the other, expulsed as soon as he tries to enter: the machine-boat, the capitalist machine of the uncle, the machine-hotel and so on. In *The Trial*, it is once again a question of a determined machine like the single machine of justice; but its unity is so nebulous, an influence machine, a contamination, that there is no longer any difference between being outside or inside. In *The Castle*, the apparent unity gives way in turn to a basic segmentation ("[The Castle was only] a rambling pile consisting of innumerable small buildings closely packed together. . . . I don't fit in with the peasants, nor, I imagine, with the Castle. 'There is no difference between the peasantry and the Castle,' said the teacher"); but this time, the indistinction of inside and outside leads to the discovery of another dimension, a sort of adjacency marked by halts, sudden stops where parts, gears, and segments assemble themselves: "The street he was in . . . did not lead up to the castle hill; it only made toward it and then, as if deliberately, turned aside, and though it did not lead away from the castle, it led no nearer to it either." Desire evidently passes through these positions and states or, rather, through all these lines. Desire is not form, but a procedure, a process.

# Chapter 2
# An Exaggerated Oedipus

Kafka's "Letter to the Father," on which so many unfortunate psychoanalytic interpretations are based is a portrait, a photo, inserted into a machine of an entirely different sort. The father with his head bent—not only because he is guilty himself, but also because he makes the son feel guilty and never stops judging him. Everything is the father's fault: if I have sexual problems, if I don't get married, if I cannot write, if I lower my head in public, if I have had to construct an alternate, infinitely more barren world. Yet this letter comes very late. Kafka knows quite well that nothing in it is true. His inaptitude for marriage, his writing, the attraction to an intense and barren world are completely positive motivations from a libidinal point of view; they aren't reactions in a derivative relation to the father. Kafka himself declares that a thousand times, and Max Brod will speak about the weakness of any Oedipal interpretation of Kafka's conflicts, even the infantile ones.[1] Nonetheless, the interest of the letter lies in a particular sliding effect; Kafka moves from a classic Oedipus of the neurotic sort, where the beloved father is hated, accused, and declared to be guilty, to a much more perverse Oedipus who falls for the hypothesis of the father's innocence, of a "distress" shared by father and son alike. But Kafka makes this move in order to engage in an even more extreme accusation, a reproach that is so strong that it becomes unattributable to any particular persons and unlimited (like the "postponement" of *The Trial*) and passes through a series of paranoid interpretations. Kafka feels it so strongly that he imagines the father speaking and he has him say: you want to show "first, that you are not guilty; second, that I am the guilty one; and third, that out of sheer magnamity, you are ready not only to forgive me but (what is both more and less) also to prove and be willing to believe yourself that—contrary to the truth—I am also not guilty." This perverse shift, which finds in the supposed innocence of the father an even worse accusation, evidently has a goal, an effect, a procedure behind it.

The goal is to obtain a blowup of the "photo," an exaggeration of it to the point of absurdity. The photo of the father, expanded beyond all bounds, will be projected onto the geographic, historical, and political *map* of the world in order to reach vast regions of it: "I feel as if I could consider living in only those regions that either are not covered by you or are not within your reach." An Oedipalization of the universe. The Name of the Father encodes the names of history—Jews, Czechs, Germans, Prague, city-county. But beyond that, to the degree that one enlarges Oedipus, this sort of microscopic enlargement shows up the father for what he is; it gives him a *molecular agitation in which an entirely different sort of combat is being played out.* One might say that in projecting the photo of the father onto the map of the world, Kafka unblocks the impasse that is specific to the photo and invents a way out of this impasse, putting it into connection with a whole underground network, and with all the ways out from this network. As Kafka himself says, the problem isn't that of liberty but of escape. The question of the father isn't how to become free in relation to him (an Oedipal question) but how to find a path there where he didn't find any. The hypothesis of a common innocence, of a distress shared by father and son, is thus the worst of all hypotheses. In it, the father appears as the man who had to renounce his own desire and his own faith, if only to leave the "rural ghetto" where he was born; he appears as the man who demands only that the son submit because he himself is in submission to a dominant order in a situation from which there is no way out ("The whole thing is, of course, no isolated phenomenon. It was much the same with a large section of this transitional generation of Jews, which had migrated from the still comparatively devout countryside to the cities"). In short, it's not Oedipus that produces neurosis; it is neurosis—*that is, a desire that is already submissive and searching to communicate its own submission*—that produces Oedipus. Oedipus, the market value of neurosis. In contrast, to augment and expand Oedipus by adding to it and making a paranoid and perverse use of it is already to escape from submission, to lift one's head up, and see passing above the shoulders of the father what had really been the question all along: an entire micropolitics of desire, of impasses and escapes, of submissions and rectifications. Opening the impasse, unblocking it. Deterritorializing Oedipus into the world instead of reterritorializing everything in Oedipus and the family. But to do this, Oedipus had to be enlarged to the point of absurdity, comedy. To do this, the "Letter to the Father" had to be written. The mistake of psychoanalysis was to trap itself and us, since it lives off of the market value of neurosis from which it gains all its surplus value. "Dramas and tragedies are written about [the revolt of the son against the father], yet in reality it is material for comedy".[2]

Two years after the "Letter to the Father," Kafka admitted that he had "plunged into discontent" and did so "with all the means that [his] time and tradition gave [him]."[3] It turns out that Oedipus is one of these means — fairly modern, widespread since Freud's time, allowing many comic effects. All it takes is to exaggerate it: "Strange how make-believe, if engaged in systematically enough, can change into reality." But Kafka does not refuse the exterior influence of the father only in order to invoke an interior genesis or an internal structure that would still be Oedipal. "I cannot grant that the first beginnings of my unhappiness were inwardly necessitated; they may have indeed had a necessity, but not an inward one — they *swarmed down on me like flies* and could have been as easily driven off." In that lies the essential point: beyond the exterior or the interior, an agitation, a molecular dance, an entire limit-connection with an Outside that is going to disguise itself as an exaggerated Oedipus that is beyond all limits.

This can occur because the comic amplification has two aspects to it. On the one hand, one discovers behind the familial triangle (father-mother-child) other infinitely more active triangles from which the family itself borrows its own power, its own drive to propagate submission, to lower the head and make heads lower. Because it's *that* that the libido of the child really invests itself in from the start: by means of the family photo, a whole map of the world. Sometimes, one of the terms of the familial triangle finds itself replaced by another term that is enough to defamiliarize the whole thing (thus, the family store stages a scene of father-employees-child with the child placing himself near the lowest of the employees whose boots he wishes to lick; or in *The Trial*, the Russian friend takes the place of one of the terms of the triangle and transforms it into a machine of judgment or condemnation). Sometimes, it's the whole triangle that changes its form and its characters and reveals itself to be judiciary or economic or bureaucratic or political, and so on. Take, for example, the judge-lawyer-accused in *The Trial* where the father no longer exists as such (or the trio of uncle-lawyer-Block who each want K at all costs to take the trial seriously). Or the proliferating trios — bank employees, policemen, judges. Or the geopolitical triangle of Germans-Czechs-Jews which is an implicit aspect of Kafka's father: "In Prague, people reproached [the Jews] for not being Czechs, and in Saaz and Eger, for not being Germans."[4] For this reason, the hypothesis of the innocence and the distress of the father forms the worst of accusations, the father having done nothing but lower his head, submit to a power that is not his own, enter into an impasse, by betraying his origin as a Czech Jew from the countryside.

Thus, the too well-formed family triangle is really only a conduit for investments of an entirely different sort that the child endlessly discovers underneath his father, inside his mother, in himself. The judges, commissioners, bureaucrats, and so on, are not substitutes for the father; rather, it is the father who is a condensation of all these forces that he submits to and that he tries to get his son to submit to. The family opens onto doors, on which from the beginning there knock " *'diabolical powers' that rejoice from the fact that they will arrive soon.*"[5] What Kafka immediately anguishes or rejoices in is not the father or the superego or some sort of signifier but the American technocratic apparatus or the Russian bureaucracy or the machinery of Fascism. And to the degree that the familial triangle comes undone either in a single term or in its totality to the profit of those *powers* that are really its driving force, we could say that the other triangles that surge up behind it have something malleable, diffuse, a perpetual transformation from one triangle to another, either because one of the terms or points begins to proliferate, or because the sides of the triangle don't stop deforming. Thus, at the beginning of *The Trial*, three unidentified characters turn into three bank employees, in a shifting relation to the three inspectors and the three curious people clustered at the window. In the first representation of the tribunal, we are still in the realm of the well-determined triangle with the judge and the two sides, right and left. But then we find an internal proliferation that spreads like a cancerous invasion, an inextricable entangling of offices and bureaucrats, an infinite and ungraspable hierarchy, a contamination of suspect spaces (although he uses entirely different means, one could find an equivalent in Proust where the unity of characters and the figures that they constitute give way to nebulae, to proliferating, fluid ensembles). Similarly, behind the father, there is all the ambiguity of the Jews, who have left their rural Czech milieu to go to the German towns, even if it means being attacked on two sides—a triangle of transformation. All children can understand this; they all have a political and geographic map with diffuse and moving contours if only because of their nursemaids, servants, employees of the father, and so on. And if the father maintains the love and admiration of his son, that's because in his childhood, the father already confronted some of the diabolical powers even if it meant being beaten by them.

Yet, insofar as the comic expansion of Oedipus allows one to see these other oppressor triangles through the lens of the microscope, there appears at the same time the possiblity of an escape, a line of escape. To the inhumaness of the "diabolical powers," there is the answer of a becoming-animal: to become a beetle, to become a dog, to become an ape, "head over heels and away," rather than lowering one's head and remaining a bureaucrat, inspector, judge, or judged. All children build or feel these sorts of escapes, these acts of becoming-animal. And the animal as an act of becoming has nothing to do with a substitute for the father, or with an archetype. Because the father, as a Jew who leaves the country to settle in the city, is undoubtedly caught in a process of real deterritorialization; but he never stops reterritorializing, in his family, in his business, in the system of his submissions and of his authorities. As for the archetypes, these are processes of spiritual reterritorialization.[6] The acts of becoming-animal are the exact opposite of this; these are absolute deterritorializations, at least in principle, that penetrate deep into the desert world invested in by Kafka. "Yet the attraction of my world too is strong; those who love me love me because I am 'forsaken'—not, I feel sure, on the principle of a Weissian vacuum, but because they sense that in happy moments I enjoy on another plane *the freedom of movement* completely lacking to me here."[7] To become animal is to participate in movement, to stake out the path of escape in all its positivity, to cross a threshold, to reach a continuum of intensities that are valuable only in themselves, to find a world of pure intensities where all forms come undone, as do all the significations, signifiers, and signifieds, to the benefit of an unformed matter of deterritorialized flux, of nonsignifying signs. Kafka's animals never refer to a mythology or to archetypes but correspond solely to new levels, zones of liberated intensities where contents free themselves from their forms as well as from their expressions, from the signifier that formalized them. There is no longer anything but movements, vibrations, thresholds in a deserted matter: animals, mice, dogs, apes, cockroaches are distinguished only by this or that threshold, this or that vibration, by the particular underground tunnel in the rhizome or the burrow. Because these tunnels are underground intensities. In the becoming-mouse, it is a whistling that pulls the music and the meaning from the words. In the becoming-ape, it is a coughing that "sound[s] dangerous but mean[s] nothing" (to become a tuberculoid ape). In the becoming-insect, it is a mournful whining that carries along the voice and blurs the resonance of words. Gregor becomes a cockroach not to flee his father but rather to find an escape where his father didn't know to find one, in order to flee the director, the business, and the bureaucrats, to reach that region where the voice no longer does anything but hum: " 'Did you hear him? It was an animal's voice,' said the chief clerk."

It is true that Kafka's animal texts are much more complex that we seem to be saying. Or, quite the contrary, much simpler. For example, in the "Report to an Academy," it is no longer a question of a becoming-animal of man, but a becoming-man of the ape; this becoming is presented as a simple imitation and if it is a question of finding an escape (an escape, and not "liberty"), this escape doesn't consist in fleeing—quite the contrary. Flight is challenged when it is useless movement in space, a movement of false liberty; but in contrast, flight is affirmed when it is a stationary flight, a flight of intensity ("No, freedom was not what I wanted. Only a way out; right, or left, or in any direction; I made no other demand"). On the other hand, the imitation is only superficial, since it no longer concerns the reproduction of figures but the production of a continuum of intensities in a nonparallel and asymmetrical evolution where the man no less becomes an ape than the ape becomes a man. The act of becoming is a capturing, a possession, a plus-value, but never a reproduction or an imitation.

"[T]here was no attraction for me in imitating human beings; I imitated them because I needed a way out, and for no other reason." In fact, the animal captured by the man finds itself deterritorialized by human force, as the whole of the beginning of "A Report" tells us. But, in turn, the deterritorialized animal force precipitates and intensifies the deterritorialization of the deterritorializing human force (if we can express it that way). "My ape nature fled out of me, head over heels and away, so that my first teacher was almost himself turned into an ape by it, had soon to give up teaching and was taken away to a mental hospital."[8] Thus, there is constituted a conjunction of the flux of deterritorialization that overflows imitation which is always territorial. It is in this way also that the orchid seems to reproduce an image of the bee but in a deeper way deterritorializes into it, at the same time that the bee in turn deterritorializes by joining with the orchid: the capture of a fragment of the code, and not the reproduction of an image. (In "The Investigations of a Dog," every idea of resemblance is even more energetically eliminated. Kafka attacks "the suspect temptations of resemblence that imagination proposes"; through the dog's solitude, it is the greatest difference, the schizo difference that he tries to grasp.)

Thus, we have two effects of the development or comic enlargement of Oedipus: the discovery *a contrario* of other triangles that operate beneath and, indeed, in the familial triangle, and the *a posteriori* outlining of paths of escape of the orphaned becoming-animal. No text seems to better show the connection of these two aspects than "The Metamorphosis." The bureaucratic triangle forms itself progressively. First, the director who comes to menace and to demand; then the father who has resumed his work at the bank and who sleeps in his uniform, demonstrating the external power that he is still in submission to as if even at home he was "only at the beck and call of his superior" and finally, in a single moment, the intrusion of the three bureaucrat lodgers who penetrate the family itself, taking up its roles, sitting "where formerly Gregor and his father and mother had taken their meals." And as a correlate of all of this, the whole becoming-animal of Gregor, his becoming beetle, junebug, dungbeetle, cockroach, which traces an intense line of flight in relation to the familial triangle but especially in relation to the bureaucratic and commercial triangle.

But at the very moment when we seemed to grasp the connections of a Going Beyond and a Falling Short of Oedipus, why are we farther than ever from a wayout; why do we remain at an impasse? It is because there is always the danger of the return of Oedipal force. The amplifying perverse usage of Oedipus is not sufficient to guard against every new closure, every new reconstitution of the familial triangle that takes over other triangles such as the animal lines. In this sense, "The Metamorphosis" is the exemplary story of a re-Oedipalization. We would say that the process of Gregor's deterritorialization through his becoming-animal finds itself blocked for a moment. Is it the fault of Gregor who doesn't dare go all the way? To please him, his sister wanted to empty out the whole room. But Gregor refused to let go of the portrait of the lady in fur. He sticks to the portrait, as if to a last territorialized image. In fact, that's what the sister cannot tolerate. She accepted Gregor; like him, she wanted the schizo incest, an incest of strong connections, incest with the sister in opposition to Oedipal incest, incest that gives evidence of a nonhuman sexuality as in the becoming-animal. But, jealous of the portrait, she begins to hate Gregor and condemns him. From that point on, Gregor's deterritorialization through the becoming-animal fails; he re-Oedipalizes himself through the apple that is thrown at him and has nothing to do but die, the apple buried in his back. Likewise, the deterritorialization of the family through more complex and diabolical triangles has no room to develop; *the father chases away the three bureaucrat lodgers*, a return to the paternalistic principle of the Oedipal triangle, the family happily closes in on itself. And yet, it is not certain that Gregor was at fault. Isn't it rather that the acts of becoming-animal cannot follow their principle all the way through — that they maintain a certain ambiguity that leads to their insufficiency and condemns them to defeat? Aren't the animals still too formed, too significative, too territorialized? Doesn't the whole of the becoming-animal oscillate between a schizo escape and an Oedipal impasse? The dog, Oedipal animal par excellence, is often referred to by Kafka in his Diaries and his letters as a schizo beast, like the musical dogs of "The Investigations," or as the diabolical dog of "Temptation in the Village." In fact, Kafka's principal animal tales were written just before *The Trial* or at the same time as it, like a sort of counterpoint to the novel which liberates itself from all animal concern to the benefit of a much higher concern.

# Chapter 3
# What Is a Minor Literature?

So far we have dealt with little more than contents and their forms: bent head–straightened head, triangles-lines of escape. And it is true that in the realm of expression, the bent head connects to the photo, and the erect head to sound. But as long as the form and the deformation or expression are not considered for themselves, there can be no real way out, even at the level of contents. Only expression gives us the *method*. The problem of expression is staked out by Kafka not in an abstract and universal fashion but in relation to those literatures that are considered minor, for example, the Jewish literature of Warsaw and Prague. A minor literature doesn't come from a minor language; it is rather that which a minority constructs within a major language. But the first characteristic of minor literature in any case is that in it language is affected with a high coefficient of deterritorialization. In this sense, Kafka marks the impasse that bars access to writing for the Jews of Prague and turns their literature into something impossible—the impossibility of not writing, the impossibility of writing in German, the impossibility of writing otherwise.[1] The impossibility of not writing because national consciousness, uncertain or oppressed, necessarily exists by means of literature ("The literary struggle has its real justification at the highest possible levels"). The impossibility of writing other than in German is for the Prague Jews the feeling of an irreducible distance from their primitive Czech territoriality. And the impossibility of writing in German is the deterritorialization of the German population itself, an oppressive minority that speaks a language cut off from the masses, like a "paper language" or an artificial language; this is all the more true for the Jews who are simultaneously a part of this minority and excluded from it, like "gypsies who have stolen a German child from its crib." In short, Prague German is a deterritorialized language, appropriate for strange and minor uses. (This can be compared in another context to what blacks in America today are able to do with the English language.)

The second characteristic of minor literatures is that everything in them is political. In major literatures, in contrast, the individual concern (familial, marital, and so on) joins with other no less individual concerns, the social milieu serving as a mere environment or a background; this is so much the case that none of these Oedipal intrigues are specifically indispensable or absolutely necessary but all become as one in a large space. Minor literature is completely different; its cramped space forces each individual intrigue to connect immediately to politics. The individual concern thus becomes all the more necessary, indispensable, magnified, because a whole other story is vibrating within it. In this way, the family triangle connects to other triangles—commercial, economic, bureaucratic, juridical—that determine its values. When Kafka indicates that one of the goals of a minor literature is the "purification of the conflict that opposes father and son and the possibility of discussing that conflict," it isn't a question of an Oedipal phantasm but of a political program. "Even though something is often thought through calmly, one still does not reach the boundary where it connects up with similar things, one reaches the boundary soonest in politics, indeed, one even strives to see it before it is there, and often sees this limiting boundary everywhere. . . . What in great literature goes on down below, constituting a not indispensable cellar of the structure, here takes place in the full light of day, what is there a matter of passing interest for a few, here absorbs everyone no less than as a matter of life and death."[2]

The third characteristic of minor literature is that in it everything takes on a collective value. Indeed, precisely because talent isn't abundant in a minor literature, there are no possibilities for an individuated enunciation that would belong to this or that "master" and that could be separated from a collective enunciation. Indeed, scarcity of talent is in fact beneficial and allows the conception of something other than a literature of masters; what each author says individually already constitutes a common action, and what he or she says or does is necessarily political, even if others aren't in agreement. The political domain has contaminated every statement (énoncé). But above all else, because collective or national consciousness is "often inactive in external life and always in the process of break-down," literature finds itself positively charged with the role and function of collective, and even revolutionary, enunciation. It is literature that produces an active solidarity in spite of skepticism; and if the writer is in the margins or completely outside his or her fragile community, this situation allows the writer all the more the possibility to express another possible community and to forge the means for another consciousness and another sensibility; just as the dog of "Investigations" calls out in his solitude to *another science*. The literary machine thus becomes the relay for a revolutionary machine-to-come, not at all for ideological reasons but because the literary machine alone is determined to fill the conditions of a collective enunciation that is lacking elsewhere in this milieu: *literature is the people's concern.*[3] It is certainly in these terms that Kafka sees the problem. The message doesn't refer back to an enunciating subject who would be its cause, no more than to a subject of the statement (*sujet d'énoncé*) who would be its effect. Undoubtedly, for a while, Kafka thought according to these traditional categories of the two subjects, the author and the hero, the narrator and the character, the dreamer and the one dreamed of.[4] But he will quickly reject the role of the narrator, just as he will refuse an author's or master's literature, despite his admiration for Goethe. Josephine the mouse renounces the individual act of singing in order to melt into the collective enunciation of "the immense crowd of the heros of [her] people." A movement from the individuated animal to the pack or to a collective multiplicity — seven canine musicians. In "The Investigations of a Dog," the expressions of the solitary researcher tend toward the assemblage (*agencement*) of a collective enunciation of the canine species even if this collectivity is no longer or not yet given. There isn't a subject; *there are only collective assemblages of enunciation*, and literature expresses these acts insofar as they're not imposed from without and insofar as they exist only as diabolical powers to come or revolutionary forces to be constructed. Kafka's solitude opens him up to everything going on in history today. The letter K no longer designates a narrator or a character but an assemblage that becomes all the more machine-like, an agent that becomes all the more collective because an individual is locked into it in his or her solitude (it is only in connection to a subject that something individual would be separable from the collective and would lead its own life).

The three characteristics of minor literature are the deterritorialization of language, the connection of the individual to a political immediacy, and the collective assemblage of enunciation. We might as well say that minor no longer designates specific literatures but the revolutionary conditions for every literature within the heart of what is called great (or established) literature. Even he who has the misfortune of being born in the country of a great literature must write in its language, just as a Czech Jew writes in German, or an Ouzbekian writes in Russian. Writing like a dog digging a hole, a rat digging its burrow. And to do that, finding his own point of underdevelopment, his own *patois*, his own third world, his own desert. There has been much discussion of the questions "What is a marginal literature?" and "What is a popular literature, a proletarian literature?" The criteria are obviously difficult to establish if one doesn't start with a more objective concept — that of minor literature. Only the possibility of setting up a minor practice of major language from within allows one to define popular literature, marginal literature, and so on.[5] Only in this way can literature really become a collective machine of expression and really be able to treat and develop its contents. Kafka emphatically declares that a minor literature is much more able to work over its material.[6] Why this machine of expression, and what is it? We know that it is in a relation of multiple deterritorializations with language; it is the situation of the Jews who have dropped the Czech language at the same time as the rural environment, but it is also the situation of the German language as a "paper language." Well, one can go even farther; one can push this movement of deterritorialization of expression even farther. But there are only two ways to do this. One way is to artificially enrich this German, to swell it up through all the resources of symbolism, of oneirism, of esoteric sense, of a hidden signifier. This is the approach of the Prague school, Gustav Meyrink and many others, including Max Brod.[7] But this attempt implies a desperate attempt at symbolic reterritorialization, based in archetypes, Kabbala, and alchemy, that accentuates its break from the people and will find its political result only in Zionism and such things as the "dream of Zion." Kafka will quickly choose the other way, or, rather, he will invent another way. He will opt for the German language of Prague as it is and in its very poverty. Go always farther in the direction of deterritorialization, to the point of sobriety. Since the language is arid, make it vibrate with a new intensity. Oppose a purely intensive usage of language to all symbolic or even significant or simply signifying usages of it. Arrive at a perfect and unformed expression, a materially intense expression. (For these two possible paths, couldn't we find the same alternatives, under other conditions, in Joyce and Beckett? As Irishmen, both of them live within the genial conditions of a minor literature. That is the glory of this sort of minor literature—to be the revolutionary force for all literature. The utilization of English and of every language in Joyce. The utilization of English and French in Beckett. But the former never stops operating by exhilaration and overdetermination and brings about all sorts of worldwide reterritorializations. The other proceeds by dryness and sobriety, a willed poverty, pushing deterritorialization to such an extreme that nothing remains but intensities.)

How many people today live in a language that is not their own? Or no longer, or not yet, even know their own and know poorly the major language that they are forced to serve? This is the problem of immigrants, and especially of their children, the problem of minorities, the problem of a minor literature, but also a problem for all of us: how to tear a minor literature away from its own language, allowing it to challenge the language and making it follow a sober revolutionary path? How to become a nomad and an immigrant and a gypsy in relation to one's own language? Kafka answers: steal the baby from its crib, walk the tightrope.

Rich or poor, each language always implies a deterritorialization of the mouth, the tongue, and the teeth. The mouth, tongue, and teeth find their primitive territoriality in food. In giving themselves over to the articulation of sounds, the mouth, tongue, and teeth deterritorialize. Thus, there is a certain disjunction between eating and speaking, and even more, despite all appearances, between eating and writing. Undoubtedly, one can write while eating more easily than one can speak while eating, but writing goes further in transforming words into things capable of competing with food. Disjunction between content and expression. To speak, and above all to write, is to fast. Kafka manifests a permanent obsession with food, and with that form of food *par excellence*, in other words, the animal or meat—an obsession with the mouth and with teeth and with large, unhealthy, or gold-capped teeth.[8] This is one of Kafka's main problems with Felice. Fasting is also a constant theme in Kafka's writings. His writings are a long history of fasts. The Hunger Artist, surveyed by butchers, ends his career next to beasts who eat their meat raw, placing the visitors before an irritating alternative. The dogs try to take over the mouth of the investigating hound by filling it with food so that he'll stop asking questions, and there too there is an irritating alternative: "[T]hey would have done better to drive me away and refuse to listen to my questions. No, they did not want to do that; they did not indeed want to listen to my questions, but it was because I asked these questions that they did not want to drive me away." The investigating hound oscillates between two sciences, that of food—a science of the Earth and of the bent head ("Whence does the Earth procure this food?")—and that of music which is a science of the air and of the straightened head, as the seven musical dogs of the beginning and the singing dog of the end well demonstrate. But between the two there is something in common, since food can come from high up and the science of food can only develop through fasting, just as the music is strangely silent.

Ordinarily, in fact, language compensates for its deterritorialization by a reterritorialization in sense. Ceasing to be the organ of one of the senses, it becomes an instrument of Sense. And it is sense, as a correct sense, that presides over the designation of sounds (the thing or the state of things that the word designates) and, as figurative sense, over the affectation of images and metaphors (those other things that words designate under certain situations or conditions). Thus, there is not only a spiritual reterritorialization of sense, but also a physical one. Similarly, language exists only through the distinction and the complementarity of a subject of enunciation, who is in connection with sense, and a subject of the statement, who is in connection, directly or metaphorically, with the designated thing. This sort of ordinary use of language can be called extensive or representative—the reterritorializing function of language (thus, the singing dog at the end of the "Investigations" forces the hero to abandon his fast, a sort of re-Oedipalization).

Now something happens: the situation of the German language in Czechoslovakia, as a fluid language intermixed with Czech and Yiddish, will allow Kafka the possibility of invention. Since things are as they are ("it is as it is, it is as it is," a formula dear to Kafka, marker of a state of facts), he will abandon sense, render it no more than implict; he will retain only the skeleton of sense, or a paper cutout.

Since articulated sound was a deterritorialized noise but one that will be reterritorialized in sense, it is now sound itself that will be deterritorialized irrevocably, absolutely. The sound or the word that traverses this new deterritorialization no longer belongs to a language of sense, even though it derives from it, nor is it an organized music or song, even though it might appear to be. We noted Gregor's warbling and the ways it blurred words, the whistling of the mouse, the cough of the ape, the pianist who doesn't play, the singer who doesn't sing and gives birth to her song out of her nonsinging, the musical dogs who are musicians in the very depths of their bodies since they don't emit any music. Everywhere, organized music is traversed by a line of abolition—just as a language of sense is traversed by a line of escape—in order to liberate a living and expressive material that speaks for itself and has no need of being put into a form.[9] This language torn from sense, conquering sense, bringing about an active neutralization of sense, no longer finds its value in anything but an accenting of the word, an inflection: "I live only here or there in a small word in whose vowel. . . . I lose my useless head for a moment. The first and last letters are the beginning and end of my fishlike emotion."[10] Children are well skilled in the exercise of repeating a word, the sense of which is only vaguely felt, in order to make it vibrate around itself (at the beginning of *The Castle*, the schoolchildren are speaking so fast that one cannot understand what they are saying). Kafka tells how, as a child, he repeated one of his father's expressions in order to make it take flight on a line of non-sense: "end of the month, end of the month"[11] The proper name, which has no sense in itself, is particularly propitious for this sort of exercise. *Milena*, with an accent on the *i*, begins by evoking "a Greek or a Roman gone astray in Bohemia, violated by Czech, cheated of its accent," and then, by a more delicate approximation, it evokes "a woman whom one carries in one's arms out of the world, out of the fire," the accent marking here an always possible fall or, on the contrary, "the lucky leap which you yourself make with your burden."[12]

It seems to us that there is a certain difference, even if relative and highly nuanced, between the two evocations of the name Milena: one still attaches itself to an extensive, figurative scene of the fantasmatic sort; the second is already much more intensive, marking a fall or a leap as a threshold of intensity contained within the name itself. In fact, we have here what happens when sense is actively neutralized. As Wagenbach says, "The word is master; it directly gives birth to the image." But how can we define this procedure? Of sense there remains only enough to direct the lines of escape. There is no longer a designation of something by means of a proper name, nor an assignation of metaphors by means of a figurative sense. But *like* images, the thing no longer forms anything but a sequence of intensive states, a ladder or a circuit for intensities that one can make race around in one sense or another, from high to low, or from low to high. The image is this very race itself; it has become becoming—the becoming-dog of the man and the becoming-man of the dog, the becoming-ape or the becoming-beetle of the man and vice versa. We are no longer in the situation of an ordinary, rich language where the word dog, for example, would directly designate an animal and would apply metaphorically to other things (so that one could say "like a dog").[13] *Diaries*, 1921: "Metaphors are one of the things that makes me despair of literature." Kafka deliberately kills all metaphor, all symbolism, all signification, no less than all designation. Metamorphosis is the contrary of metaphor. There is no longer any proper sense or figurative sense, but only a distribution of states that is part of the range of the word. The thing and other things are no longer anything but intensities overrun by deterritorialized sound or words that are following their line of escape. It is no longer a question of a resemblance between the comportment of an animal and that of a man; it is even less a question of a simple wordplay. There is no longer man or animal, since each deterritorializes the other, in a conjunction of flux, in a continuum of reversible intensities. Instead, it is now a question of a becoming that includes the maximum of difference as a difference of intensity, the crossing of a barrier, a rising or a falling, a bending or an erecting, an accent on the word. The animal does not speak "like" a man but pulls from the language tonalities lacking in signification; the words themselves are not "like" the animals but in their own way climb about, bark and roam around, being properly linguistic dogs, insects, or mice.[14] To make the sequences vibrate, to open the word onto unexpected internal intensities—in short, an asignifying *intensive utilization* of language. Furthermore, there is no longer a subject of the enunciation, nor a subject of the statement. It is no longer the subject of the statement who is a dog, with the subject of the enunciation remaining "like" a man; it is no longer the subject of enunciation who is "like" a beetle, the subject of the statement remaining a man. Rather, there is a circuit of states that forms a mutual becoming, in the heart of a necessarily multiple or collective assemblage.

How does the situation of the German language in Prague—a withered vocabulary, an incorrect syntax—contribute to such a utilization? Generally, we might call the linguistic elements, however varied they may be, that express the "internal tensions of a language" *intensives* or *tensors*. It is in this sense that the linguist Vidal Sephiha terms intensive "any linguistic tool that allows a move toward the limit of a notion or a surpassing of it," marking a movement of language toward its extremes, toward a reversible beyond or before.[15] Sephiha well shows the variety of such elements which can be all sorts of master-words, verbs, or prepositions that assume all sorts of senses; prenominal or purely intensive verbs as in Hebrew; conjunctions, exclamations, adverbs; and *terms that connote pain*.[16] One could equally cite the accents that are interior to words, their discordant function. And it would seem that the language of a minor literature particularly develops these tensors or these intensives. In the lovely pages where he analyzes the Prague German that was influenced by Czech, Wagenbach cites as the characteristics of this form of German the incorrect use of prepositions; the abuse of the pronominal; the employment of malleable verbs (such as *Giben*, which is used for the series "put, sit, place, take away" and which thereby becomes intensive); the multiplication and succession of adverbs; the use of pain-filled connotations; the importance of the accent as a tension internal to the word; and the distribution of consonants and vowels as part of an internal discordance. Wagenbach insists on this point: all these marks of the poverty of a language show up in Kafka but have been taken over by a creative utilization for the purposes of a new sobriety, a new expressivity, a new flexibility, a new intensity.[17] "Almost every word I write jars up against the next, I hear the consonants rub leadenly against each other and the vowels sing an accompaniment like Negroes in a minstrel show."[18] *Language stops being representative in order to now move toward its extremities or its limits.* The connotation of pain accompanies this metamorphosis, as in the words that become a painful warbling with Gregor, or in Franz's cry "single and irrevocable." Think about the utilization of French as a spoken language in the films of Godard. There too is an accumulation of stereotypical adverbs and conjunctions that form the base of all the phrases—a strange poverty that makes French a minor language within French; a creative process that directly links the word to the image; a technique that surges up at the end of sequences in connection with the intensity of the limit "that's enough, enough, he's had enough," and a generalized intensification, coinciding with a panning shot where the camera pivots and sweeps around without leaving the spot, making the image vibrate.

Perhaps the comparative study of images would be less interesting than the study of the functions of language that can work in the same group across different languages—bilingualism or even multilingualism. Because the study of the functions in distinct languages alone can account for social factors, relations of force, diverse centers of power, it escapes from the "informational" myth in order to evaluate the hierarchic and imperative system of language as a transmission of orders, an exercise of power or of resistance to this exercise. Using the research of Ferguson and Gumperz, Henri Gobard has proposed a tetralinguistic model: vernacular, maternal, or territorial language, used in rural communities or rural in its origins; a vehicular, urban, governmental, even worldwide language, a language of businesses, commercial exchange, bureaucratic transmission, and so on, a language of the first sort of deterritorialization; referential language, language of sense and of culture, entailing a cultural reterritorialization; mythic language, on the horizon of cultures, caught up a spiritual or religious reterritorialization. The spatiotemporal categories of these languages differ sharply: vernacular language is *here*; vehicular language is *everywhere*; referential language is *over there*; mythic language is *beyond*. But above all else, the distribution of these languages varies from one group to the next and, in a single group, from one epoch to the next (for a long time in Europe, Latin was a vehicular language before becoming referential, then mythic; English has become the worldwide vehicular language for today's world).[19] What can be said in one language cannot be said in another, and the totality of what can and can't be said varies necessarily with each language and with the connections between these languages.[20] Moreover, all these factors can have ambiguous edges, changing borders, that differ for this or that material. One language can fill a certain function for one material and another function for another material. Each function of a language divides up in turn and carries with it multiple centers of power. A blur of languages, and not at all a system of languages. We can understand the indignation of integrationists who cry when Mass is said in French, since Latin is being robbed of its mythic function. But the classicists are even more behind the times and cry because Latin has even been robbed of its referential cultural function. They express regret in this way for the religious or educational forms of powers that this language exercised and that have now been replaced by other forms. There are even more serious examples that cross over between groups. The revival of regionalisms, with a reterritorialization through dialect or patois, a vernacular language — how does that serve a worldwide or transnational technocracy? How can that contribute to revolutionary movements, since they are also filled with archaisms that they are trying to impart a contemporary sense to? From Servan-Schreiber to the Breton bard to the Canadian singer. And that's not really how the borders divide up, since the Canadian singer can also bring about the most reactionary, the most Oedipal of reterritorializations, oh mama, oh my native land, my cabin, olé, olé. We would call this a blur, a mixed-up history, a political situation, but linguists don't know about this, don't want to know about this, since, as linguists, they are "apolitical," pure scientists. Even Chomsky compensated for his scientific apoliticism only by his courageous struggle against the war in Vietnam.

Let's return to the situation in the Hapsburg empire. The breakdown and fall of the empire increases the crisis, accentuates everywhere movements of deterritorialization, and invites all sorts of complex reterritorializations — archaic, mythic, or symbolist. At random, we can cite the following among Kafka's contemporaries: Einstein and his deterritorialization of the representation of the universe (Einstein teaches in Prague, and the physicist Philipp Frank gives conferences there with Kafka in attendance); the Austrian dodecaphonists and their deterritorialization of musical representation (the cry that is Marie's death in *Wozzeck*, or Lulu's, or the echoed *si* that seems to us to follow a musical path similar in certain ways to what Kafka is doing); the expressionist cinema and its double movement of deterritorialization and reterritorialization of the image (Robert Wiene, who has Czech background; Fritz Lang, born in Vienna; Paul Wegener and his utilization of Prague themes). Of course, we should mention

Viennese psychoanalysis and Prague school linguistics.[21] What is the specific situation of the Prague Jews in relation to the "four languages?" The vernacular language for these Jews who have come from a rural milieu is Czech, but the Czech language tends to be forgotten and repressed; as for Yiddish, it is often disdained or viewed with suspicion — it *frightens*, as Kafka tells us. German is the vehicular language of the towns, a bureaucratic language of the state, a commercial language of exchange (but English has already started to become indispensable for this purpose). The German language — but this time, Goethe's German — has a cultural and referential function (as does French to a lesser degree). As a mythic language, Hebrew is connected with the start of Zionism and still possesses the quality of an active dream. For each of these languages, we need to evaluate the degrees of territoriality, deterritorialization, and reterritorialization. Kafka's own situation: he is one of the few Jewish writers in Prague to understand and speak Czech (and this language will have a great importance in his relationship with Milena). German plays precisely the double role of vehicular and cultural language, with Goethe always on the horizon (Kafka also knows French, Italian, and probably a bit of English). He will not learn Hebrew until later. What is complicated is Kafka's relation to Yiddish; he sees it less as a sort of linguistic territoriality for the Jews than as a nomadic movement of deterritorialization that reworks German language. What fascinates him in Yiddish is less a language of a religious community than that of a popular theater (he will become patron and impresario for the travelling theater of Isak Lowy).[22] The manner in which Kafka, in a public meeting, presented Yiddish to a rather hostile Jewish bourgeois audience is completely remarkable: Yiddish is a language that frightens more than it invites disdain, "dread mingled with a certain fundamental distaste"; it is a language that is lacking a grammar and that is filled with vocables that are fleeting, mobilized, emigrating, and turned into nomads that interiorize "relations of force." It is a language that is grafted onto Middle-High German and that so reworks the German language from within that one cannot translate it into German without destroying it; one can understand Yiddish only by "feeling it" in the heart. In short, it is a language where minor utilizations will carry you away: "Then you will come to feel the true unity of Yiddish and so strongly that it will frighten you, yet it will no longer be fear of Yiddish but of yourselves. Enjoy this self-confidence as much as you can!"[23]

Kafka does not opt for a reterritorialization through the Czech language. Nor toward a hypercultural usage of German with all sorts of oneiric or symbolic or mythic flights (even Hebrew-ifying ones), as was the case with the Prague school. Nor toward an oral, popular Yiddish. Instead, using the path that Yiddish opens up to him, he takes it in such a way as to convert it into a unique and solitary form of writing. Since Prague German is deterritorialized to several degrees, he will always take it farther, to a greater degree of intensity, but in the direction of a new sobriety, a new and unexpected modification, a pitiless rectification, a straightening of the head. Schizo politeness, a drunkenness caused by water.[24] He will make the German language take flight on a line of escape. He will feed himself on abstinence; he will tear out of Prague German all the qualities of underdevelopment that it has tried to hide; he will make it cry with an extremely sober and rigorous cry. He will pull from it the barking of the dog, the cough of the ape, and the bustling of the beetle. He will turn syntax into a cry that will embrace the rigid syntax of this dried-up German. He will push it toward a deterritorialization that will no longer be saved by culture or by myth, that will be an absolute deterritorialization, even if it is slow, sticky, coagulated. To bring language slowly and progressively to the desert. To use syntax in order to cry, to give a syntax to the cry.

There is nothing that is major or revolutionary exept the minor. To hate all languages of masters. Kafka's fascination for servants and employees (the same thing in Proust in relation to servants, to their language). What interests him even more is the possibility of making of his own language—assuming that it is unique, that it is a major language or has been—a minor utilization. To be a sort of stranger *within* his own language; this is the situation of Kafka's Great Swimmer.[25] Even when it is unique, a language remains a mixture, a schizophrenic mélange, a Harlequin costume in which very different functions of language and distinct centers of power are played out, blurring what can be said and what can't be said; one function will be played off against the other, all the degrees of territoriality and relative deterritorialization will be played out. Even when major, a language is open to an intensive utilization that makes it take flight along creative lines of escape which, no matter how slowly, no matter how cautiously, can now form an absolute deterritorialization. All this inventiveness, not only lexically, since the lexical matters little, but sober syntactical invention, simply to write like a dog (but a dog can't write—exactly, exactly). It's what Artaud did with French—cries, gasps; what Celine did with French, following another line, one that was exclamatory to the highest degree. Celine's syntactic evolution went from *Voyage* to *Death on the Credit Plan*, then from *Death on the Credit Plan* to *Guignol's Band*. (After that, Celine had nothing more to talk about except his own misfortunes; in other words, he had no longer any desire to write, only the need to make money. And it always ends like that, language's lines of escape: silence, the interrupted, the interminable, or even worse. But until that point, what a crazy creation, what a writing machine! Celine was so applauded for *Voyage* that he went even further in *Death on the Credit Plan* and then in the prodigious *Guignol's Band* where language is nothing more than intensities. He spoke with a kind of "minor music." Kafka, too, is a minor music, a different one, but always made up of deterritorialized sounds, a language that moves head over heels and away.) These are the true minor authors. An escape for language, for music, for writing. What we call pop—pop music, pop philosophy, pop writing—Worterflucht. To make use of the polylingualism of one's own language, to make a minor or intensive use of it, to oppose the oppressed quality of this language to its oppressive quality, to find points of nonculture or under-development, linguistic Third World zones by which a language can escape, an animal enters into things, an assemblage comes into play. How many styles or genres or literary movements, even very small ones, have only one single dream: to assume a major function in language, to offer themselves as a sort of state language, an official language (for example, psychoanalysis today, which would like to be a master of the signifier, of metaphor, of wordplay). Create the opposite dream: know how to create a becoming-minor. (Is there a hope for philosophy, which for a long time has been an official, referential genre? Let us profit from this moment in which antiphilosophy is trying to be a language of power.)

# Chapter 4
# The Components of Expression

We started with some simple formal oppositions: bent head–straightened head for the form of content, photo-sound for the form of expression. These were states or figures of desire. But it seems that sound doesn't act like a formal element; rather, it leads to an active disorganization of expression and, by reaction, of content itself. Thus, through its way of "taking flight," sound brings into play a new figure of the straightened head that now moves "head over heels and away." And far from the animal being only on the side of the bent head (or of the alimentary mouth), this same sound, this same tonality, induces a becoming-animal and links it with the restraightened head. Thus, we find ourselves not in front of a structural correspondence between two sorts of forms, forms of content and forms of expression, but rather in front of an *expression machine* capable of disorganizing its own forms, and of disorganizing its forms of contents, in order to liberate pure contents that mix with expressions in a single intense matter. A major, or established, literature follows a vector that goes from content to expression. Since content is presented in a given form of the content, one must find, discover, or see the form of expression that goes with it. That which conceptualizes well expresses itself. But a minor, or revolutionary, literature begins by expressing itself and doesn't conceptualize until afterward ("I do not see the word at all, I invent it")[1] Expression must break forms, encourage ruptures and new sproutings. When a form is broken, one must reconstruct the content that will necessarily be part of a rupture in the order of things. To take over, to anticipate, the material. "Art is a mirror, which goes 'fast,' like a watch — sometimes."[2]

What are the components of this literary machine, of Kafka's writing, or expression, machine?

One component is the letters. In what ways do they belong to the oeuvre? In fact, Kafka's work is not defined by a publishing intention. Kafka evidently did not think of publishing his letters; quite the contrary, he thought of destroying everything he wrote as though it were all like letters. If the letters really are a part of the work, it is because they are an indispensable gear, a motor part for the literary machine as Kafka conceives of it even if this machine is destined to disappear or explode to a degree comparable to the machine of the Penal Colony. Impossible to conceive of Kafka's machine without it involving an epistolary aspect. Perhaps it is as a function of the letters, of their demands, of their potentials and their insufficiencies, that the other pieces will be assembled. The fascination of Kafka for the letters of his predecessors (Flaubert, Kleist, Hebbel). But what Kafka sees and experiments on to his own ends is a perverse, diabolical utilization of the letter. "Diabolical in all its innocence," says Kafka. The letters pose directly, innocently, the diabolical power of the literary machine. To fabricate letters, this not a question of sincerity but one of functioning. Letters to this or that woman, letters to friends, letter to the father; nonetheless, there is always a woman behind these letters who is the real addressee (*destinataire*)—the woman that the father is supposed to have made him lose, the one that his friends hope he will break from, and so on. To substitute for love the letter of love?. To deterritorialize love. To substitute for the feared conjugal contract a pact with the devil. The letters are inseparable from such a pact; they are this pact itself. How to "attach girls to oneself by writing"?[3] Kafka has just made the acquaintance of the daughter of the concierge at the Goethe house in Weimar; they take photographs together, they write postcards to each other. Kafka is astonished that the girl writes to him "as he desires" and yet doesn't take him seriously, treats him "as a mere figurehead." Everything is already here in this letter, even though it hasn't reached its point of perfection. The reference to Goethe—if Kafka so admired Goethe, was this as a "master" or as the author of the pact with the devil that Faust makes and that determines the fate of Marguerite? The elements of the literary machine are already in these letters, even if they are insufficiently utilized and remain ineffective: the clichéd photo on the postcard, the writing on the reverse side, the sound that takes flight and whose intensity one reads in a lowered voice, in a single tone. In his first meeting with Felice, Kafka will show her these photos, these postcards of Weimar, as though they would serve to extablish a new circuit where matters would become more serious.

The letters are a rhizome, a network, a spider's web. There is a vampirism in the letters, a vampirism that is specifically epistolary. Dracula the vegetarian, the hunger artist, who drinks the blood of carnivorous humans, has his castle nearby. There is something of Dracula in Kafka, a Dracula who works by letters, letters that are like bats. They prowl by night and, by day, are locked in his coffin-desk: "The night is not nocturnal enough." When he imagines a kiss, it is that of Gregor who grabs onto the naked neck of his sister, or that of K with Fraulein Burstner, a kiss like that of "some thirsty animal lapping greedily at a spring of long-sought fresh water." To Felice, Kafka describes himself without shame or joke as extraordinarily thin, needing blood (my heart "is so weak that it doesn't even manage to send blood all the way to the end of my legs"). Kafka-Dracula has his line of escape in his room, in his bed, and his faraway force comes from that which the letters will bring him. He fears only two things: the family's cross and marriage's garlic. The letters must bring him blood, and the blood will give him the force to create. He is not looking for a feminine inspiration or for a maternal protection but for a physical force that will enable him to write. He says that literary creation is "payment for the devil's services." Kafka does not live the thinness of his anorexic body as shameful; he is only pretending. He understands his body as the means while in bed to cross thresholds and acts of becoming, each organ "being under special observation." All that is necessary is that one give him a little blood. A flux of letters for a flux of blood. From the first meeting with Felice, Kafka the vegetarian is attracted by her muscular arms, rich with blood, astounded by her great carnivorous teeth; Felice has a feeling of danger and assures him that she is a light eater. But from his contemplation of her, Kafka makes the decision to write, to write a great deal to Felice.[4] The letters to Milena—that will be another story. That is a more mannered kind of love, with marriage on the horizon. Kafka has learned a great deal, experimented a lot. There is in Milena an Angel of Death as Kafka himself suggests. She is more an accomplice than a recipient of a letter. Kafka explains to her the damnation of the letters, their necessary connection to a ghost who drinks up all the kisses given to him along his journey. "Dislocation of souls." And Kafka distinguishes two series of technical inventions: those that tend to restore natural communication by triumphing over distances and bringing people together (the train, the car, the airplane), and those that represent the vampirish revenge of the phantom where there is reintroduced "the ghostly element between people" (the post, the telegraph, the telephone, wireless telegraphy).[5]

But how do the letters function? Without a doubt, because of their genre, they maintain the duality of the two subjects: for the moment, let us distinguish a subject of enunciation as the form of expression that writes the letter, and a subject of the statement that is the form of content that the letter is speaking about (even if *I* speak about *me*). It is this duality that Kafka wants to put to a perverse or diabolical use. Instead of the subject of enunciation using the letter to recount his own situation, it is the subject of the statement that will take on a whole movement that has become fictive or no more than superficial. It is the sending of the letter, the trajectory of the letter, the gestures of the postman that will take the place of the subject of enunciation's recounting (hence, the importance of the postman or the messenger who is doubled, like the two messengers in *The Castle*, by the clothes that stick to him like sheets of paper). An example of a truly Kafkaesque love: a man falls for a woman that he saw only a single time; tons of letters; he can never visit; he keeps the letters close to him in a trunk; and the day after the breakup, with the last letter arriving in the country, he knocks the mailman down. The correspondence with Felice is filled with this impossibility of visiting. The flux of letters replaces seeing, arriving. Kafka never stops writing to Felice even though he's seen her only once. With all his force, he wants to impose the conditions of a pact. She must write two times a day. That's the pact with the devil. The Faustian pact with the devil finds its source in a faraway force as against the proximity of a conjugal contract. To utter things from the start and then to see only those things later on or in a dream. Kafka sees in a dream: "The whole staircase was littered from top to bottom with the loosely heaped pages I had read. That was a real wish-dream."[6] A mad desire to write and to tear the letters away from their addressee. Given their generic nature, the desire of the letters thus consists of the following: it transfers movement onto the subject of the statement; it gives the subject of the statement an apparent movement, an unreal movement, that spares the subject of enunciation all need for a real movement. As in "Wedding Preparations," this subject can remain on his pallet, like an insect, since he has sent his fully-dressed double in the letter, with the letter. This exchange, or this reversal of the duality of the two subjects, the subject of the statement taking on that real movement that is normally the province of the subject of the enunciation, produces a doubling. And it is this doubling that is already diabolical; the devil is this very doubling. Here, we find one of the origins of the double in Kafka: "The Man Who Disappeared," the first draft of *Amerika*, which portrays two brothers "one of whom [goes] to America while the other remain[s] in a European prison."[7] And "The Verdict," which revolves entirely around the theme of letters, portrays the subject of enunciation who remains in the paternal store and the Russian friend who is not only an addressee but a potential subject of the statement and *who does not exist perhaps outside the letters*.

Letters as a minor genre, letters as desire, the desire of letters, have a second generic characteristic. That which is the greatest horror for the subject of enunciation will be presented as an external obstacle that the subject of the statement, relegated to the letter, will try at all costs to conquer, even if it means perishing. That is called "The Description of a Struggle." The horror of Kafka toward all forms of conjugality. A prodigious operation by which he translates this horror into a *topography of obstacles* (where to go? how to arrive? Prague, Vienna, Berlin?). The Surveyor. And also the other operation by which he enumerates a numbered *list of conditions* that the subject of the statement thinks can dissipate horror when, in fact, it is this very horror in the subject of enunciation that inspires them (a Life Plan or a Life Program, à la Kleist). It is really torturous, it is the embodiment of the humors. A double and dark reversal of the stages of romantic love and of marriage. This method comports several advantages. It allows one to posit the innocence of the subject of enunciation, since he can do nothing and has done nothing; the innocence also of the subject of the statement, since he has done everything possible; and even the innocence of the third party, of the addressee (even you, Felice, you are innocent). And finally this method makes things worse than they would be if only one of these instances, or the entire world, was guilty. This is the method that triumphs in the "Letter to the Father." Everyone is innocent, that is the worst of possibilities. The "Letter to the Father" is the exorcism of Oedipus and the family by the writing machine, just as the letters to Felice are the exorcism of conjugality. *To make a map of Thebes instead of performing Sophocles, to make a topography of obstacles instead of fighting against destiny* (to substitute a destined addressee for destiny). It is useless to ask whether the letters are a part of the oeuvre or whether they are the source of some of the themes of the work; they are an integrative part of the writing machine or the expression machine. It is as such that we must think of the letters in general as belonging to the writing, outside the work or not, and understand moreover why certain literary forms such as the novel have naturally made use of the epistolary form.

But there is a third generic characteristic: this function of the letters doesn't immediately prevent a superficial return of guilt. An Oedipal, familial, or conjugal return of guilt. Am I capable of loving my father? Am I able to get married? Am I a monster? "Devilish in [one's] innocence," one can be innocent and yet diabolical. This is the theme of "The Judgment" and the constant sentiment that Kafka feels in his relationships with the women he loves.[8] He knows that he is Dracula and he knows that he is a vampire, a spider and its web. Only it is more than ever necessary to distinguish various points—the duality of the two subjects, their exchange or their doubling, *seem* to found a feeling of guilt. But, there again, the guilty one is ultimately the subject of the statement. The guilt itself is only the surface movement, an ostentatious movement, that hides an intimate laugh (how many awful things have been written on Kafka and guilt, Kafka and the law, and so on). Judaism, a paper envelope: Dracula cannot feel guilty, Kafka cannot feel guilty, Faust is not guilty, and this is not a bit of hypocrisy. The heart of the matter lies elsewhere. One cannot understand anything about a diabolical pact, a pact with the devil, if one believes that it can inspire guilt in the person who signs it, that is, the one who initiates it or writes the letter. Guilt is the statement of a judgment that comes from outside and that works, preys, only on a weak soul. Weakness, oh my weakness, my fault, guilt is a surface movement in Kafka as a subject of the statement. In contrast, there is his force as a subject of enunciation in the desert. But that doesn't solve anything, one is not saved for that. Because if guilt is only a surface movement, it is brandished precisely as the index of an entirely different danger—the other affair. The real panic is that the writing machine will turn against the mechanic. Look at the Penal Colony. The danger of the diabolical pact, of diabolical innocence, is not guilt but the trap, the impasse within the rhizome, the closing of all escape, the burrow that is blocked everywhere. *Fear*. The devil himself is caught in the trap. One allows oneself to be re-Oedipalized not by guilt but by fatigue, by a lack of invention, by the imprudence of what one has started, by the photo, by the police—diabolical powers from faraway. Thus innocence no longer matters. The formula of diabolical innocence saves you from guilt but does not save you from the photocopy of the pact and the condemnation that results from it. The danger is not feeling guilt as a neurosis, as a state, but judging guilt as a Trial. And that's the fatal outcome of the letter; the "letter to the father" is a trial that closes in on Kafka; the letters to Felice turn into a mock Trial, with an entire tribunal, family, friends, defense, accusation. Kafka has a presentiment of this from the start, since he is writing "The Judgment" at the same time he begins the letters to Felice. But "The Judgment" comes from the great fear that a letter machine will entrap the author. The father begins by denying that the addressee, the Russian friend, exists; then he recognizes his existence, but only to reveal that the friend has been writing to him (the father) in order to denounce the son's betrayal (the flux of the letters changes direction; it turns back on its sender; and so on). "Your ugly little letters . . . " The "ugly letter" of Sortini, the bureaucrat, in *The Castle*. To wish away this new danger, Kafka never stops confusing matters; he sends yet another letter that modifies or denies what he's just sent so that Felice will always be one letter behind in her replies. But nothing stops the return of destiny: in his rupture with Felice, Kafka will emerge broken, but not guilty. He for whom these letters were an indispensable component, a positive (not negative) instigation to write everything, finds himself without a desire to write, his whole body broken by the trap that almost caught him. The formula, "devilish in innocence," hasn't been enough.

[These three intensive elements show why Kafka was fascinated by letters. You have to have a special sensibility for that. At this point, we would like to compare his letters to those of another diabolical figure, Proust. Proust also uses his letters to make a faraway pact with the devil or a phantom in order to break the proximity of the conjugal contract. He too opposes writing and marriage. Two scrawny and anorexic vampires who take nourishment from blood only by sending out their letter-bats. The overall principle is the same in both cases: each letter is a letter of love, whether real or superficial. Love letters can be attractive, repulsive, or filled with reproach, compromise, or proposition, without any of that changing anything about their nature; they are part of a pact with the devil that wishes away the contract with God, with the family, or with the loved one. But, more precisely, the first quality of the letters—an exchange or doubling of the two subjects—appears fully in Proust: the subject of the statement assumes all the movement while the subject of the enunciation remains in bed, in a corner of his web like a spider (Proust's becoming-spider). Moreover, topographies of obstacles and lists of conditions as functions of the letter are given priority in Proust to such a degree that the addressee can't tell if the author wants him to come visit, has never wanted that, is pushing the addressee away only to really tempt the addressee, and so on. The letter loses its identity as a memory, dream, or photo to become a rigorous map of the paths to take or to avoid, a rigidly conditioned life program (like *The Castle*, Proust's work is the complicated path of a road that never stops approaching while moving away).[9] Finally, as in Kafka, guilt in Proust is only a superficial envelope that accompanies the argument or the apparent motion of the subject of the statement; but beneath this playful guilt, there is deeper panic in the recumbent writer—fear that he's said too much, fear that the letter machine will turn against him and throw him back into what he was trying to get rid of, anguish that the many little messages or the dirty little letters will entrap him. The incredible blackmail letter to Albertine that he sends when he doesn't know that she is dead and that comes back to him in the form of a special delivery message from Gilberte, whom he confuses with Albertine, announcing her marriage. He too will emerge broken from all this. But with an equivalent vampirism, with an equivalent jealousy. The differences between Proust and Kafka are great and involve more than the difference between the worldly, diplomatic style of the former and the investigative, judicial style of the latter. Both of them seek to avoid, through letters, the specific sort of proximity that characterizes the conjugal relationship and turns the situation into a seeing and being seen (fo example, Kafka's terror when Felice tells him that she would like to be near him while he works). It doesn't matter whether the conjugality is official or unofficial, heterosexual or homosexual. But to get rid of proximity, Kafka maintains and guards spatial distance, the faraway position of the loved one: he too presents himself as a prisoner (prisoner of his body, of his room, of his family, of his oeuvre) and multiplies the obstacles that prevent him from seeing or rejoining his beloved.[10] In Proust, in contrast, the same exorcism takes place in an inverse way: one reaches the imperceptible, the invisible, by exaggerating proximity, by making it a carceral proximity. Proust's solution is the strangest—to overcome the conjugal conditions of presence and of vision. By an excessive rapprochement. One sees less the closer one is. Thus, it is Proust who is the *jailer* while the loved one is in a contiguous prison. The ideal of Proust's letters consists of small notes slid under the door.]

Another component of Kafka's writing machine is the stories. They are essentially animalistic even though there aren't animals in all the stories. According to Kafka, the animal is the object *par excellence* of the story: to try to find a way out, to trace a line of escape. The letters aren't enough, since the devil, the pact with the devil, not only offers no line of escape but risks making us fall into a trap. Kafka writes stories like "The Judgment" or "The Metamorphosis" at the same time that he begins the correspondence with Felice, either to give an image of the danger or to exorcise it—better to have finished and mortal stories than the infinite flux of letters. The letters are perhaps the motor force that, by the blood they collect, start the whole machine working. Nonetheless, for Kafka, it is a question of writing something other than letters—a question, then, of creating. This something other is presaged by the letters (the animal nature of the victim, that is, of Felice, vampirish utilization of the letters themselves) but can only be realized in an autonomous writing even if it remains perpetually unachieved. What Kafka does in his room is to become animal and this is the essential object of the stories. The first sort of creation is the metamorphosis. A wife's eyes shouldn't see that above all else, nor should the eyes of a father or mother. We would say that for Kafka, the animal essence is the way out, the line of escape, even if it takes place in place, or in a cage. *A line of escape, and not freedom. A vital escape and not an attack.* In "The Jackals and the Arabs," the jackals say, "We're not proposing to kill them. . . . Why, the mere sight of their living flesh makes us turn tail and flee into cleaner air, into the desert, which for that very reason is our home." If Bachelard is unfair to Kafka when he compares him to Lautreamont, this is because he assumes above all else that the dynamic essence of the animal lies in freedom and aggression: Madoror's becomings-animal are attacks that are all the more cruel in being free and gratuitous. It is not like this in Kafka; it is the exact opposite, and we could even say that his concept is the more correct one from the point of view of Nature itself. Bachelard's postulate leads him to oppose Lautreamont's speed and Kafka's slowness.[11] Let us remind ourselves, however, of several elements of the animalistic stories: (1) there is no possibility of distinguishing those cases where the animal is treated as an animal and those where it is part of a metamorphosis; everthing in the animal is a metamorphosis, and the metamorphosis is part of a single circuit of the becoming-human of the animal and the becoming-animal of the human; (2) the metamorphosis is a sort of conjunction of two deterritorializations, that which the human imposes on the animal by forcing it to flee or to serve the human, but also that which the animal proposes to the human by indicating ways-out or means of escape that the human would never have thought of by himself (schizo-escape); each of these two deterritorializations is immanent to the other and makes it cross a threshold; (3) thus, what matters is not at all the relative slowness of the becoming-animal; because no matter how slow it is, and even the more slow it is, it constitutes no less an *absolute deterritorialization* of the man in opposition to the merely relative deterritorializations that the man causes to himself by shifting, by traveling; the becoming-animal is an immobile voyage that stays in one place; it only lives and is comprehensible as an intensity (to transgress the thresholds of intensity).[12]

There is nothing metaphoric about the becoming-animal. No symbolism, no allegory. Nor is it the result of a flaw or a malediction, the effect of some sort of guilt. As Melville says of the becoming-whale of Captain Ahab, it is a "pano-rama," not a "Gospel." It is a map of intensities. It is an ensemble of states, each distinct from the other, grafted onto the man insofar as he is searching for a way out. It is a creative line of escape that says nothing other than what it is. In con-trast to the letters, the becoming-animal lets nothing remain of the duality of a subject of enunciation and a subject of the statement; rather, it constitutes a sin-gle process, a unique method that replaces subjectivity. However, if the becoming-animal is the object par excellence of the stories, we must in turn ex-amine the insufficiencies of the the stories. We might say that they are caught up in a choice that from both sides condemns them to defeat from the point of view of Kafka's project, no matter their literary splendor. On the one hand, the story will be perfect and finished but then will close in on itself. Or it will open but will open to something that could only be developed in a novel that would be itself interminable. In the first case, the story confronts a danger that is different from that of the letters, although somewhat analogous. The letters had to fear a sort of reflux directed against the subject of enunciation; the stories, on the other hand, bump up against a no-way out of the animal way out, an impasse of the line of escape (it is for this reason that they end when they erect this im-passe). To be sure, the becoming-animal has nothing to do with a merely super-ficial sort of meaning, like that in the letters: however slow it may be, the deter-ritorialization of the becoming-animal is absolute; the line of escape is well programmed, the way out is well established. But this is only one side of the poles. In the same way that the egg, in its potentiality, contains two poles, the becoming-animal is a potentiality that is gifted with two equally real poles—a properly animal pole and a properly familial one. We saw how the animal oscil-lated between its own becoming-inhuman and an all-too-human familiarization: thus, the dog in "The Investigations" is deterritorialized by the musical dogs at the story's beginning, but he is reterritorialized, re-Oedipalized, by the singer-dog of the ending. He ends up oscillating between two "sciences" and is reduced to invoking the eventual coming of a third science that would manage to escape the situation (but, obviously, this third science will no longer be the object of a mere story and will demand a whole novel). To take another example: we saw how Gregor's metamorphosis was the story of a re-Oedipalization that leads him into death, that turns his becoming-animal into a becoming-dead. Not only the dog, but all the animals, oscillate between a schizo Eros and an Oedipal Thanatos. It is in this perspective alone that metaphor, with its whole an-thropocentric entourage, threatens to come back on the scene. In short, the animalist stories are a component of the machine of expression, but distinct from the letters, since they no longer operate within a superficial movement or within the distinction of two subjects. Grasping the real, writing themselves within the real itself, they are caught up in the tension between two opposing poles or reali-ties. The becoming-animal effectively shows a way out, traces a line of escape, but is incapable of following it or making it its own (for this reason, "The Judgment" remains an Oedipal story, one that Kafka presents as such, where the son dies without becoming an animal and without being able to develop an open contact with Russia).

Thus, we have to consider the other hypothesis: not only do the animal stories show a way out that the becomings-animal are themselves incapable of following, but already, that which enabled them to show the way out was something different that acted inside them. And this something different can be really expressed only in the novels, in the attempts at novels, as the third component of the machine of expression. Because in the exact moment Kafka begins the novels (or tries to expand a story into a novel) he abandons the becomings-animal in order to substitute for them a more complex assemblage. The stories and their becomings-animal had already been inspired by this underground assemblage, but they weren't able to make this assemblage function directly—they weren't even able to make it see the light of day. It was as though the animal was still too close, still too perceptible, too visible, too individuated, and so the becoming-animal started to become a *becoming-molecular*: Josephine the mouse surrounded by her people, "the numberless throng of the heroes of our people," the perplexed dog in front of the agitation in all directions of the seven musical dogs; the confused animal of "The Burrow" faced with the thousands of sounds that came from all sides from undoubtedly smaller animals; the hero of "Memoirs of the Kalda Railroad," who came to hunt bear and wolves, but who found only rat packs that he killed with a knife while watching them wave their little hands (and in "The Bucket Rider," "In the thick, hard-frozen snow, I walk along the tracks of small arctic dogs, my movement has lost all direction"). Kafka is fascinated by everything that is small. If he doesn't seem to like children that is because they are caught in an irreversible becoming-big; the animal kingdom, in contrast, involves smallness and imperceptibility. But, even more, in Kafka, the molecular multiplicity tends itself to become integrated with, or make room for, a machine, or rather a *machinic assemblage*, the parts of which are independent of each other, but which functions nonetheless. The grouping of the musical dogs is actually described as this sort of very minute assemblage. Even when the animal is unique, its burrow isn't; the burrow is a multiplicity and an assemblage. The Blumfeld story presents a bachelor who begins by asking himself if he should get a little dog; but the relaying of the dog is determined by a strange molecular or machinic system, "two small white celluloid balls with blue stripes jumping up and down side by side on the parquet." Blumfeld is finally persecuted by two subordinate assistants who act as parts of a bureaucratic machine. Maybe there is in Kafka a very particular intermediary situation, since he himself exists between still being an animal and already being an assemblage. In any case, the animals, as they are or become in the stories, are caught in this alternative: either they are beaten down, caught in an impasse, and the story ends; or, on the contrary, they open up and multiply, digging new ways out all over the place but giving way to molecular multiplicities and to machinic assemblages that are no longer animal and can only be given proper treatment in the novels.

The novels are the third component of Kafka's writing machine. They present very few animals, except in secondary roles, and no becoming-animal. It is as though the negative pole of the animal had been neutralized and the positive pole, for its part, had emigrated elsewhere, to the realm of the machine and assemblages. It is as though the becoming-animal was not rich enough in articulations and junctions. Let us imagine that Kafka wrote a novel about the bureaucratic world of ants or about the Castle of the termites: in that case, he would have been a sort of Capek (a compatriot and contemporary of Kafka). He would have written a science fiction novel. Or a dark novel, a realist novel, an idealist novel, a roman-à-clef—genres that one could find in the Prague school. He would have described, more or less directly, more or less symbolically, the modern world, the sadness or the rigidity of this world, the crimes of mechanicity and of bureaucracy. None of these things were part of Kafka's writing project. Had he written about the justice of the ants or the castle of the termites, the whole realm of metaphors, realist or symbolist, would have returned. He would never have been able to so sharply grasp the violence of an Eros that is bureaucratic, judiciary, economic, or political.

Someone might say that the break we are instituting between the stories and the novels doesn't exist, since many of the stories are drafts, disjointed building blocks for eventually abandoned novels, and that the novels in turn are interminable and unfinished stories. But that's not the question. The question is: what makes Kafka plan for a novel and, renouncing it, abandon it or try to close it up in the form of story, or, on the other hand, say to himself that maybe a story can be the starting-point for a novel even if it will also be abandoned? We could propose the following sort of rule (of course, it doesn't always apply; it works only in some cases): (1) when a text deals essentially with a becoming-animal, it cannot be developed into a novel; (2) a text that deals with a becoming-animal cannot be thought to be developable into a novel except if it also includes sufficient machinic indexes that go beyond the animal and that, in this way, are the seeds for a novel; (3) a text that can be the seed of a novel will be abandoned if Kafka imagines an animal escape that allows him to finish with it; (4) a novel doesn't become a novel, even if it is unfinished, even and especially if it is interminable, unless the machinic indexes organize themselves into a real assemblage that is self-sufficient; (5) on the other hand, a text that includes an explicit machine will not develop unless it succeeds in plugging into a concrete sociopolitical assemblage (since a pure machine is only a blueprint that forms neither a story nor a novel). Kafka thus has many reasons to abandon a text, either because it stops short or because it is interminable. But Kafka's criteria are of an entirely new sort and apply only to him; from one genre of text to another, there are interactions, reinvestments, exchanges, and so on. Each failure is a masterpiece, a branch of the rhizome.

The first case would apply to "The Metamorphosis". This is why many critics say that it is the most perfected (?) of Kafka's works. Given over to his becoming-animal, Gregor finds himself re-Oedipalized by his family and goes to his death. The family even stifles the potentialities of a bureaucratic machine (as with the three tenants who are chased away). The story ends then in a state of mortuary perfection. The second case could apply to "The Investigations of a Hound." Kafka sees it as his own sort of *Bouvard et Pecuchet*.[13] But the seeds of development that are effectively present here are inseparable from the machinic indexes that give rhythm to the object of the "Investigations"—the musical indexes of the assemblage of the seven dogs, the scientific indexes of the three forms of knowledge. But since these indexes are still caught in and by the becoming-animal, they abort. Kafka will not succeed here in writing his *Bouvard et Pecuchet*; this is because the dogs put him on the path of something *that he can grasp only through another sort of material*. The third case is illustrated by "The Penal Colony." There too the seed of a novel exists, connected this time to an explicit machine. But this machine, which is too mechanical, still too connected to overly Oedipal coordinates (the commandant-officer=father-son), doesn't develop at all. And Kafka can imagine an animal conclusion to this text that falls back to the level of a story: in one version of the "Colony," the voyager finally becomes a dog and starts running in all directions on all fours, leaping around and hurrying back to his post (in another version a snake-woman intervenes).[14] This is the inverse of "The Investigations of a Hound"; instead of the machinic indexes suceeding in escaping from the becoming-animal, the machine reverts to a new rebecoming-animal. The fourth case, which is the only really positive one, concerns the three big novels, the three big interminable works: here, the machine is no longer mechanical and reified; instead, it is incarnated in very complicated social assemblages that, through the employment of human personnel, through the use of human parts and cogs, realize effects of inhuman violence and desire that are infinitely stronger than those one can obtain with animals or with isolated mechanisms. This is why it is important to observe how at a single moment (for example, the moment of *The Trial*), Kafka continues to describe becomings-animal that are not developed into novels and conceives of a novel that never stops developing its assemblages. The fifth and last case would be a sort of counter proof of this: there is a "defeat" in the novel not only when the becoming-animal continues to predominate but also when the machine doesn't succeed in incarnating itself in the living political and social assemblages that make up the animated material of the novel. In this case, the novel remains a rough draft that also cannot develop, no matter what its force and beauty may be. This is already true of "The Penal Colony" with its still too transcendental, too isolated and reified, and too abstract machine. It is also true of the admirable, three page text "The Cares of a Family Man," which describes a strange and useless machine: "a flatstar-shaped spool, around which is wound broken-off bits of thread [and] that is traversed by a small wooden crossbar . . . and another small rod is joined to that at a right angle." It is also true in the case of Blumfeld where the two ping-pong balls form a pure machine, the two perverse and idiotic subordinate assistants form a bureaucratic assemblage, even though these themes remain disjointed and the writing jumps from one to the other without each one diffusing and penetrating the other.

Here, then, are the three elements of the machine of writing or of expression insofar as they are defined by internal criteria, and not by a publishing project. The letters and the diabolical pact; the stories and the becoming-animal; the novels and the machinic assemblages. Between these three elements, there is constant transversal communication, in one direction and another. The Felice who appears in the letters is an animal not only insofar as, by her sanguinary nature, she is a choice-prey for the vampire, but even more because there is in her a full becoming-dog that fascinates Kafka. And, as a modern machinic assemblage, *The Trial* itself refers back to reactualized archaic sources—a trial of the becoming-animal that comes to include the condemnation of Gregor, a trial of the vampire because of his diabolical pact, a condemnation that Kafka really lived when he first broke up with Felice, like the trial in the hotel where he compared everything to being in front of a tribunal. Nonetheless, we should not believe that there is only one line that extends from the lived experience of the letters to the written experience of the stories and the novels. There is also a reverse path, and there is an equal amount of lived and written experience in both situations. Thus, it is the trial as a social, political, and juridical assemblage that causes Kafka to grasp his becomings-animal, one by one, as the material in a trial, and to treat his epistolary relationship with Felice as one to be judged within the terms of a trial. Moreover, the path doesn't go only from the diabolical pact of the letters to the becoming-animal of the stories. It also takes on an opposite meaning; the becomings-animal have value only in terms of the assemblages that inspire them—assemblages where the animals function like pieces of a musical machine or of a science machine, a bureaucratic machine, and so on, and so on. And the letters are already part of a machinic assemblage where fluxes are exchanged and where the postman plays the erotic role of an indispensable cog of the machine, a bureaucratic mediator without whom the epistolary pact would be unable to operate (when the dream postman brings Felice's letters, "He delivered them to me, one in each hand, his arms moving in perfect precision, like the jerking of piston rods in a steam engine."[15]) There is a perpetual communication between the three components of expression. And although the communication is interrupted in each case in its own way, it is also passed from component to component. Letters that are stopped because a return,

THE COMPONENTS OF EXPRESSION □ 41

a processing, blocks them; stories that stop because they cannot develop into novels, torn in two directions that block any way out—another processing; novels that Kafka himself stops, since they are interminable and essentially unlimited, infinite—a third trial. Never has so complete an oeuvre been made from movements that are always aborted, yet always in communication with each other. Everywhere there is a single and unique passion for writing but not the same one. Each time the writing crosses a threshold; and there is no higher or lower threshold. These are thresholds of intensities that are not higher or lower than the sound that runs through them.

That's why it is so awful, so grotesque, to oppose life and writing in Kafka, to suppose that he took refuge in writing out of some sort of lack, weakness, impotence, in front of life. A rhizome, a burrow, yes—but not an ivory tower. A line of escape, yes—but not a refuge. The creative line of escape vacuums up in its movement all politics, all economy, all bureaucracy, all judiciary: it sucks them like a vampire in order to make them render still unknown sounds that come from the near future—Fascism, Stalinism, Americanism, *diabolical powers that are knocking at the door*. Because expression precedes content and draws it along (on the condition, of course, is nonsignifying): living and writing, art and life, are opposed only from the point of view of a major literature. Even when he is dying, Kafka is overrun by a flux of invincible life that comes equally from his letters, his stories, his novels—from their individual incompletion (for whatever reason) and their ability to communicate with each other, to be exchangeable. Conditions of a minor literature. Only one thing really bothers Kafka and angers him, makes him indignant: when people treat him as a writer of intimacy, finding a refuge in literature, as an author of solitude, of guilt, of an intimate misfortune. However, that's really Kafka's fault, since he held out that interpretation in order to anticipate the trap through his humor. There is a Kafka laughter, a very joyous laughter, that people usually understand poorly. It is for stupid reasons that people have tried to see a refuge far from life in Kafka's literature, and also an agony, the mark of an impotence and a culpability, the sign of a sad interior tragedy. Only two principles are necessary to accord with Kafka. He is an author who laughs with a profound joy, a *joie de vivre*, in spite of, or because of, his clownish declarations that he offers like a trap or a circus. And from one end to the other, he is a political author, prophet of the future world, because he has two poles that he will know how to unify in a completely new assemblage: far from being a writer withdrawn into his room, Kafka finds that his room offers him a double flux, that of a bureaucrat with a great future ahead of him, plugged into real assemblages that are in the process of coming into shape, and that of a nomad who is involved in fleeing things in the most contemporary way and who plugs into socialism, anarchism, social movements.[16] Writing for Kafka, the primacy of writing, signifies only one thing: not a form of literature alone, the enunciation forms a unity with desire, beyond laws, states, regimes. Yet the enunciation is always historical, political, and social. A micropolitics, a politics of desire that questions all situations. Never has there been a more comic and joyous author from the point of view of desire; never has there been a more political and social author from the point of view of enunciation. Everything leads to laughter, starting with *The Trial*. Everything is political, starting with the letters to Felice.

# Chapter 5
# Immanence and Desire

Negative theology (or the theology of absence), the transcendence of the law, the a prioriness of guilt are the dominant themes of so much Kafka interpretation. The famous passages in *The Trial* (as well as in "The Penal Colony" and "The Great Wall of China") present the law as a pure and empty form without content, the object of which remains unknowable: thus, the law can be expressed only through a sentence, and the sentence can be learned only through a punishment. No one knows the law's interior. No one knows what the law is in the Colony; and the needles of the machine write the sentence on the body of the condemned, who doesn't know the law, at the same time as they inflict their torture upon him. "He will learn [the sentence] on his body." In "The Great Wall of China": "[I]t is an extremely painful thing to be ruled by laws that one does not know. . . . [T]he essence of a secret code is that it should remain a mystery." Kant constructed a rational theory of the law's reversal from a Greek conception to the Judeo-Christian one. The law no longer depends on a preexistent Good that would give it a materiality; it is a pure form on which the good such as it is depends. The good is that which the law expresses when it expresses itself. One might say that Kafka situates himself as part of this reversal. But the humor that he puts into it shows an entirely different intention. For him, it is less a question of presenting this image of a transcendental and unknowable law than of *dissecting the mechanism* of an entirely different sort of machine, which needs this image of the law only to align its gears and make them function together with "a perfect synchronicity" (as soon as this image-photo disappears, the pieces of the machine disperse as in "The Penal Colony"). *The Trial* must be considered a scientific investigation, a report of the experiments on the functioning of a machine in which the law runs the strong risk of playing no more than the role of exterior armature. That's why the texts in *The Trial* should be used only with great care. The primary problem has involved misjudging the relative importance of these texts and making unwarranted assumptions about their placement in the novel, as is expecially evident in the ways that Max Brod arranged things to support his thesis of negative theology.

Two chapters are of particular concern: the brief final chapter, about K's execution, and the preceding chapter, "In the Cathedral," in which the priest represents the discourse of the law. Nothing tells us that the final chapter was written at the end of *The Trial*; it might have been written when Kafka had just begun to revise and was still under the influence of his breakup with Felice. It is a premature, delayed, aborted ending. One can't fix the place where Kafka would have put it. It might well be a dream that could fit anywhere in the course of the novel. Indeed, Kafka published, by itself and under the title "A Dream," another fragment originally envisioned for *The Trial*. Max Brod is thus better inspired when he notes the degree to which *The Trial* is an interminable novel, necessarily indefinite: "But as the trial, according to the author's own statement made by word of mouth, was never to get as far as the highest Court, in a certain sense the novel could never be terminated — that is to say, it could be prolonged into infinity" (postface to *The Trial*. Trans. Willa and Edwin Muir. [New York: Alfred A. Knopf, 1956], 334). The idea of ending with K's execution is contradicted by the whole direction of the novel and by the quality of "unlimited postponement" that regulates *The Trial*. The imposition of K's execution as the final chapter seems to have an equivalent in the history of literature — the placement of the famous description of the plague at the end of Lucretius's book. In both cases, it is a question of showing that at the last moment, an epicurian can do no more than submit to agony, or that a Prague Jew can only assume the guilt that is operating within him. As for the other chapter, "In the Cathedral," the place of honor given to it, as though it indicated some sort of key to the novel, as though it constituted proof of the book's religious character, is also well contradicted by its own content. The story about the gatekeeper of the law remains highly ambiguous, and K learns that the priest who tells this story is a member of the judiciary apparatus, chaplain for the prisons, one element in a whole series of other elements, and that he has no privilege, since the series has no need to stop with him. We agree with Uyttersprot's proposal to remove this chapter and put it before that entitled "The Lawyer, the Industrialist, and the Painter."[1]

From the point of view of a supposed transcendence of the law, there must be a certain necessary connection of the law with guilt, with the unknowable, with the sentence or the utterance. Guilt must in fact be the a priori that corresponds to transcendence, for each person or for everyone, guilty or innocent. Having no object and being only pure form, the law cannot be a domain of knowledge but is exclusively the domain of an absolute practical necessity: the priest in the cathedral explains that "it is not necessary to accept everything as true, one must only accept it as necessary." Finally, because it has no object of knowledge, the law is operative only in being stated and is stated only in the act of punishment: a statement directly inscribed on the real, on the body and the flesh; a practical statement opposed to any sort of speculative proposition. All these themes are well presented in *The Trial*. But it is precisely these themes that will be the object of a dismantling (*démontage*), and even of a demolition, throughout Kafka's long experimentation. The first aspect of this dismantling consists in "eliminating any idea of guilt from the start," this being part of the accusation itself: culpability is never anything but the superficial movement whereby judges and even lawyers confine you in order to prevent you from engaging in a real movement—that is, from taking care of your own affairs.[2] Second, K will realize that even if the law remains unrecognizable, this is not because it is hidden by its transcendence, but simply because it is always denuded of any interiority: it is always in the office next door, or behind the door, on to infinity (we can already see this quite well in the first chapter of *The Trial* where everything happens in the "room next door"). Finally, it is not the law that is stated *because* of the demands of a hidden transcendence; it is almost the exact opposite: it is the statement, the enunciation, that constructs the law in the name of an immanent power of the one who enounces it—the law is confused with that which the guardian utters, and the writings precede the law, rather than being the necessary and derived expression of it.

The three worst themes in many interpretations of Kafka are the transcendence of the law, the interiority of guilt, the subjectivity of enunciation. They are connected to all the stupidities that have been written about allegory, metaphor, and symbolism in Kafka. And also, the idea of the tragic, of the internal drama, of the intimate tribunal, and so on. No doubt, Kafka holds out the bait. He holds it out even, and especially, to Oedipus; not from complacency but because he wants to make a very special use of Oedipus to serve his diabolical project. It is absolutely useless to look for a theme in a writer if one hasn't asked exactly what its importance is in the work—that is, *how it functions* (and not what its "sense" is). Law, guilt, interiority—Kafka has a great need for them as the superficial movement of his work. Superficial movement doesn't mean a mask underneath which something else would be hidden. The superficial movement indicates points of undoing, of dismantling, that must guide the experimentation to show the molecular movements and the machinic assemblages of which the superficial movement is a global result. We could say that law, guilt, interiority are everywhere. But all that is necessary is to consider a specific piece of the writing machine—for example, the three pricipal gears—letters, stories, novels—in order to see that these themes are really nowhere present and don't function at all. Each of these gears certainly has a primary affective tonality.

But, in the letters, it is fear, not guilt: fear of the trap that is closing in on it, fear of a return of flux, the vampire's fear of being surprised in full daylight by the sun, by religion, by garlic, and by the stake through the heart (Kafka is greatly afraid, in his letters, of people and what can happen because of them; this is quite different from guilt or humiliation). And in the stories about a becoming-animal, it is escape that has an affective tonality apart from any connection to guilt and also distinct from fear; the becoming-animal lives a life of escape more than one of fear (the animal in "The Burrow" isn't really afraid, and the jackals aren't afraid — they liverather in a sort of "lunatic hope"; the musical dogs "that could dare achieve such thing had no need to fear such things"). In the novels, finally, it is strange to see the degree to which K doesn't feel any guilt and doesn't feel fear and doesn't flee; he is completely audacious and he offers a new tonality that is very strange, a sense of dismantling that is simultaneously that of a judge and that of an engineer, a veritable feeling, a *Gemut*. Fear, flight, dismantling — we should think of them as three passions, three intensities, corresponding to the diabolical pact, to the becoming-animal, to the machinic and collective assemblages.

So, should we support realist and social interpretations of Kafka? Certainly, since they are infinitely closer to noninterpretation. And it is much more worthwhile to talk about the problems of minor literature, about the situation of a Jew in Prague, about America, about bureaucracies and about great trials, than to talk about an absent God. One could object that Kafka's America is unreal, that the New York strike remains intangible, that the most difficult working conditions receive no indignation in his work, that the election of the judge falls into the realm of pure nonsense. One might correctly note that there is never any criticism in Kafka. Even in "The Great Wall of China," the minority party can even believe that the law is only an arbitrary fact of the "nobility"; the party expresses no anger, and "that is the real reason why the parties who believe tht there is no law have remained so few — although their doctrine is in certain ways so attractive, for it unequivocally recognizes the nobility and its right to go on existing." In *The Trial*, K doesn't attack the law and willingly aligns himself with the strong side and the executioners: he prods Franz who is being whipped; he terrorizes an accused person by seizing him by the arm; at the lawyer's, he makes fun of Block. In *The Castle*, K likes to menace and punish whenever he can. Can we conclude that, not being a "critic of his time," Kafka turned his criticism "against himself" and had no other tribunal than an "internal tribunal"? This would be grotesque, since it would turn criticism into a dimension of representation. If representation is not external, it can be only internal from here on. But it's really something else in Kafka: Kafka attempts to extract from social representations assemblages of enunciation and machinic assemblages and to dismantle these assemblages. Already in the animal stories, Kafka was drawing lines of escape; but he didn't "flee the world." Rather, it was the world and its representation that he *made take flight* and that he made follow these lines. It was a question of seeing and speaking like a beetle, like a dung beetle. Even more, in the novels, the dismantling of the assemblages makes the social representation take flight in a much more effective way than a critique would have done and brings about a deterritorialization of the world that is itself political and that has nothing to do with an activity of intimacy.[3]

Writing has a double function: to translate everything into assemblages and to dismantle the assemblages. The two are the same thing. This is why we have been distinguishing in Kafka's work instances that are in fact enmeshed in each other—first, *machinic indexes*; then, *abstract machines*; and finally, *the assemblages of the machine*. The machinic indexes are the signs of an assemblage that has not yet been established or dismantled because one knows only the individual pieces that go into making it up, but not how they go together. Most frequently, these pieces are living beings, animals, but they are only valuable as moving pieces or configurations of an assemblage that goes beyond them, and whose mystery remains because they are only the operators or executors of this assemblage. Thus, the musical dogs are actually pieces of the musical assemblage and produce a cacaphony by "the lifting and setting down of their feet, certain turns of the head, their running and their standing still, the position which they [take] up in relation to one another." But they function only as indexes, since they "[do] not speak, they [do] not sing, they remain generally silent, almost determinedly silent." These machinic indexes (which are not at all allegorical or symbolical) are particularly well developed in the acts of the becoming-animal and in the animalistic stories. "The Metamorphosis" forms a complex assemblage in which the index-elements are Gregor-animal and the musical sister; in which the index-objects are the food, the sound, the photo, and the apple; and in which the index configurations are the familial triangle and the bureaucratic triangle. The bent head that straightens up and the sound that latches onto the voice and derails it also function as indexes of this sort in the majority of the stories. There is thus a machinic index each time a machine is being built and is beginning to function, even though one doesn't know how the disparate parts that make it up and make it work actually function. But the reverse case also appears in the stories: abstract machines surge into existence by themselves, without indexes. But in this case, they don't function, or no longer function. Such is the machine in the Penal Colony that answers to the Law of the old warden and doesn't survive its own dismantling; such is the creature named Odradek about whom "one is tempted to believe that the creature once had some sort of intelligible shape and is now only a broken-down remnant. Yet this does not seem to be the case . . . [T]he whole thing looks senseless enough but in its own way perfectly finished"; such too are Blumfeld's ping-pong balls. Yet it seems also that the representation of the transcendental law, with its elements of guilt and unknowability, is an abstract machine of this sort. If the machine of the Penal

Colony, as representative of the law, appears to be archaic and outmoded, this is not because, as people have often claimed, there is a new law that is much more modern but because the form of the law in general is inseparable from an abstract, self-destructive machine and cannot develop in a concrete way. This is why the stories seem to encounter two dangers that make them stop short or force them to remain incomplete or prevent them from developing into novels: either they are nothing more than machinic indexes of the assembly, no matter how lively they appear to be; or they put into operation abstract machines that are all assembled, but dead, and never succeed in concretely plugging into things (we should note that Kafka willingly publishes his texts on transcendental law in short stories that he detaches from the whole).

Thus there remain machinic assemblages as objects of the novel. This time the machinic indexes stop being animal; they group, give birth to series, start proliferating, taking over all sorts of human figures or parts of figures. On the other hand, the abstract machine changes in a singular fashion. It stops being reified and isolated; it no longer exists outside the concrete, socio-political assemblages that incarnate it. It diffuses into them and measures their machinic degree. Finally, the assemblage no longer works as a machine in the process of assembling itself, with a mysterious function, or as a fully assembled machine that doesn't function, or no longer functions. It works only through the dismantling *(démontage)* that it brings about on the machine and on representation. And, actually functioning, it functions only through and because of its own dismantling. It is born from this dismantling (it is never the assembling of the machine that interests Kafka). This method of active dismantling doesn't make use of criticism that is still part of representation. Rather, it consists in prolonging, in accelerating, a whole movement that already is traversing the social field. It operates in a virtuality that is already real without yet being actual (the diabolical powers of the future that for the moment are only brushing up against the door). The assemblage appears not in a still encoded and territorial criticism but in a decoding, in a deterritorialization, and in the novelistic acceleration of this decoding and this deterritorialization (as was the case with the German language – to always go farther in this movement that takes over the whole social field). This method is much more intense than any critique. K says so himself. One's goal is to transform what is still only a *method (procédé)* in the social field into a *procedure* as an infinite virtual movement that at the extreme invokes the machinic assemblage of the *trial (procès)* as a reality that is on its way and already there.[4] The whole of this operation is to be called a Process, one that is precisely interminable. Marthe Robert underlines the link between the trial and the procedure, and this is certainly not a mental, psychical, or interior procedure.

Here, then, are the new characteristics of the novelistic machinic assemblage in opposition to the indexes and the abstract machines. These characteristics im-

pose not an interpretation or a social representation of Kafka but an experimentation, a socio-political investigation. Since the assemblage functions really in the
real, the question becomes: how does it function? What function does it have?
(Only later will we ask what it consists of and what its elements and its links
are.) Thus, we must follow the movement of *The Trial* at several levels, taking
account of objective uncertainty about the supposed last chapter and of the cer-
tainty that the second-to-last chapter, "In the Cathedral" was more or less poorly
placed by Max Brod. According to a first view, everything is false in *The Trial*:
even the law, in contrast to Kantian law, erects the lie into a universal rule. The
lawyers are false lawyers, the judges are false judges, "oafish inspectors," "corrupt warders," or at the very least are so much subalterns that they hide the real
matters and "the proceedings of an inaccessible justice" that no longer lets itself
be represented. Nonetheless, if this first view is not definitive, this is because
there is a power in the false, and it is bad to weigh justice in terms of true or
false. So the second view is much more important: *where one believed there was
the law, there is in fact desire and desire alone.* Justice is desire and not law.
Everyone in fact is a functionary of justice—not only the spectators, not only
the priest and the painter, but also the equivocal young women and the perverse
little girls who take up so much space in *The Trial*. K's book in the cathedral
is not a prayerbook but an album of the town; the judge's book contains only
obscene pictures. The law is written in a porno book. Here, it is no longer a
question of suggesting an eventual falsity of justice but of suggesting its desiring
quality: the accused are in principle the most handsome figures and are recognized for their strange beauty. The judges act and reason "like children." It happens that a simple joke can derout repression. Justice is not Necessity but, quite
the contrary, Chance; and Titorelli paints the allegory of it as a blind fortune,
a winged desire. It is not a stable will but a moving desire. It is curious, K says,
how justice must not move in order to not sway its scales. But the priest explains
at another moment, "The Court wants nothing from you. *It receives you when
you come and dismisses you when you go.*" The young women are not equivocal
because they hide their nature as auxiliaries of justice; on the contrary, they
show themselves to be auxiliaries because they simultaneously bring bliss to
judges, lawyers, and accused, out of a single and unique polyvocal desire. The
whole of *The Trial* is overrun by a polyvocality of desire that gives it its erotic
force. Repression doesn't belong to justice unless it is also desire itself—desire
in the one who is repressed as well as in the one who represses. And the authorities of justice are not those who look for offenses but those who are "*attracted,
propelled by offense.*" They nose around, they rummage about, they search
everywhere. They are blind and accept no evidence but take into consideration
only hallway events, the whispers of the courtroom, the secrets of the chambers,
the noise heard behind doors, the murmurs from behind the scene, all those
microevents that express desire and its arbitrary fortunes.

If justice doesn't let itself be represented, that is because it is desire. Desire could never be on a stage where it would sometimes appear like a party opposed to another party (desire against the law), sometimes like the presence of the two sides under the effect of a superior law that would govern their distribution and their combination. Think of tragic representation as presented by Hegel: Antigone and Creon move on stage as if they were two parties. It is in this way that K still thinks of justice at his first interrogation. There would be two sides, two parties, one a little more favorable to desire, the other to the law, and whose distribution would refer to a superior law. But K notices that it isn't really like that: the important thing is not what happens in the tribunal or the movements of the two parties together but the molecular agitations that put into motion the hallways, the wings, the back doors, and the side chambers. The theater in *Amerika* is no more than an immense wing, an immense hallway, that has abolished all spectacle and all representation. And the same thing happens in the political realm (K himself compares the tribunal scene to a political meeting, and, more specifically, to a meeting of socialists). There also the important thing is not what happens in the tribunal where people debate only questions of ideology. Indeed, the law is one of these debated questions; everywhere in Kafka—in *The Trial*, in "The Great Wall of China"—the law is examined in terms of its connection to the parties that the different commentators belong to. But politically, the important things are always taking place elsewhere, in the hallways of the congress, behind-the-scenes of the meeting, where people confront the real, immanent problems of desire and of power—the real problem of justice.

From this point on, it is even more important to renounce the idea of a transcendence of the law. If the ultimate instances are inaccessible and cannot be represented, this occurs not as a function of an infinite hierarchy belonging to a negative theology but as a function of a *contiguity of desire* that causes whatever happens to happen always in the office next door. The contiguity of the offices, the segmentalization of power, replaces the hierarchy of instances and the eminence of the sovereign (already, the castle had revealed itself to be a segmental and contiguous rambling assemblage in the style of the Hapsburg bureaucracy or the mosaic of nations in the Austrian empire). If everything, everyone, is part of justice, if everyone is an auxiliary of justice, from the priest to the little girls, this is not because of the transcendence of the law but because of the immanence of desire. This is the discovery into which K's investigation and experimentation very quickly locks itself. While the Uncle pushes him to take his trial seriously, for example, to see a lawyer and pass through all the steps of transcendence, K realizes that he should not let himself be represented, that he has no need of a representative—that no one should come between him and his desire. He will find justice only by moving, by going from room to room, by following his desire. He will take control of the machine of expression: he will take over the investigation, he will write without stop, he will demand a leave of absence so he can totally devote himself to this "virtually interminable" work. It is in this sense that *The Trial* is an interminable novel. *An unlimited field of immanence instead of an infinite transcendence.* The transcendence of the law was an image, a photo of the highest places; but justice is more like a sound (the statement) that never stops taking flight. *The transcendence of the law was an abstract machine, but the law exists only in the immanence of the machinic assemblage of justice.* *The Trial* is the dismantling of all transcendental justifications. There is nothing to judge vis-à-vis desire; the judge himself is completely shaped by desire. Justice is no more than the immanent process of desire. The process is itself a continuum, but a continuum made up of contiguities. The contiguous is not opposed to the continuous — quite the contrary, it is a local and indefinitely prolongable version of the continuous. Thus, it is also the dismantling of the continuous — always an office next door, always the contiguous room. Barnabas "is admitted into certain rooms, but they're only a part of the whole, for there are barriers behind which there are more rooms. Not that he's actually forbidden to pass the barriers. . . . And you musn't imagine that these barriers are a definite dividing-line. . . . [T]here are barriers he can pass, and they're just the same as the ones he's never yet passed." Justice is the continuum of desire, with shifting limits that are always displaced.

It is this procedure, this continuum, this field of immanence that the painter, Titorelli, analyzes as unlimited postponement. A central part of *The Trial* that makes Titorelli into a special character of the novel. He distinguishes three theoretical possibilities: definite acquittal, ostensible or superficial acquittal, and unlimited postponement. The first case never in fact comes about, since it would imply the death or abolition of a desire that would have reached a conclusion. On the other hand, the second case corresponds to the abstract machine of law. It is defined, in fact, by the opposition of fluxes, the alternation of poles, the succession of periods — a counterflux of the law in response to a flux of desire, a pole of escape in response to a pole of repression, a period of crisis for a period of compromise. We could say that the formal law sometimes retreats into a transcendence by leaving a field provisionally open to desire, or sometimes makes the transcendence emanate hierarchized hypostases that are capable of halting and repressing desire (in fact, there are many neo-Platonic readings of Kafka). In two different ways, this state, or rather this cycle of superficial acquittal, corresponds to Kafka's situation in the letters or in the animalistic stories or in the becomings-animal. The trial at the hotel is the counterblow of the law reacting to the blow of the letters, a trial of the vampire who well knows that any acquittal can be only superficial. And succeeding the positive pole of the line of escape, the trial of the becoming-animal is the negative pole of the transcendental law that blocks the way out and that dispatches a familial hypostasis to retrap the guilty party — the re-Oedipalization of Gregor, the platonic apple that his father throws at him.

But this apple is precisely the same one that K eats at the beginning of *The Trial* as part of a broken chain that finds its link in "The Metamorphosis." Because the whole story of K revolves around the way in which he enters more deeply into an unlimited postponement, breaking with all the formulas of a superficial acquittal. He thereby leaves the abstract machine of the law that opposes law to desire, as body is opposed to spirit, as form is opposed to matter, in order to enter into the machinic assemblage of justice — that is, into the mutual immanence of a decoded law and a deterritorialized desire. But what do the terms postponement and unlimited signify? If K refuses a superficial acquittal, this is not because of a desire for a real acquittal, and even less because of an intimate hopelessness coming from a guilt that feeds off itself. Guilt is entirely on the side of a superficial acquittal. We could say that superficial acquittal is simultaneously infinite, limited, discontinuous. It is infinite because it is circular, closely following "the circulation of the offices" along the path of a large circle. But it is limited and discontinuous because the point of accusation approaches and recedes in relation to this circulation, "swinging backwards and forwards with greater or smaller oscillations, longer or shorter delays": opposed fluxes, opposed poles, opposed periods of innocence, *guilt*, freedom, and a new arrest. Since real acquittal is out of the question, the question of innocence "or" guilt falls entirely within the realm of the superficial acquittal that determines the two discontinuous periods and the reversal of one into the other. Innocence, moreover, is a hypothesis that is much more perverse than that of guilt. Innocent or guilty, this is the question of the infinite; it is certainly not the kind of question that Kafka raises. In contrast, the postponement is finite, unlimited, and continuous. It is finite because these is no longer any transcendence and because it works by means of segments; the accused no longer has to undergo "strain and agitation" or fear an abrupt reversal (no doubt, a circulation remains, but "only in the small circle to which it has been artifically restricted," and this little circulation is only "ostensible," a residue of the apparent acquittal). Also, the delay is unlimited and continuous because it doesn't stop adding one segment to the other, in contact with the other, contiguous to the other, operating piece by piece in order to always push the limit farther back. The crisis is continuous because it is always on the side that it takes place. "Contact" with justice, contiguity, have replaced the hierarchy of the law. The delay is perfectly positive and active — it goes along with the undoing of the machine, with the composition of the assemblage, always one piece next to another. It is the process in itself, the tracing of the field of immanence.[5] And it is even more evident in *The Castle* to what degree K is nothing but desire: a single problem, to establish or maintain "contact" with the Castle, to establish or maintain a "liaison."

# Chapter 6
# Proliferation of Series

This functioning of the assemblage can be explained only if one takes it apart to examine both the elements that make it up and the nature of its linkages. The characters in *The Trial* appear as part of a large series that never stops proliferating. Everyone is in fact a functionary or a representative of justice (and in *The Castle*, everyone has something to do with the castle), not only the judges, the lawyers, the bailiffs, the policemen, even the accused, but also the women, the little girls, Titorelli the painter, K himself. Furthermore, the large series subdivides into subseries. And each of these subseries has its own sort of unlimited schizophrenic proliferation. Thus, Block simultaneously employs six lawyers, and even that's not enough; Titorelli produces a series of completely identical paintings; and in all of his adventures, K meets curious young women of the same type (Elsa, his girlfriend before the trial, waitress in a cabaret; Miss Burstner, "a typist who would not resist him for very long"; the washerwoman, the judge's lover and wife to the bailiff; Leni, the nursemaid-secretary of the lawyer; and the little girls at Titorelli's place). But the first characteristic of these proliferating series is that they work to unblock a situation that had closed elsewhere in an impasse.

Doubles and trios are frequently used by Kafka. They remain distinct from each other. The triangulation of the subject, familial in origin, consists in fixing one's *position* in relation to the two other represented terms (father-mother-child). The doubling of the subject, as subject of enunciation and as subject of the statement, concerns the *movement* of the subject in one of its two representatives or in both together: sometimes it is more fraternal—based on shame—than paternal; sometimes more professional—based on rivalry—than familial. The majority of Kafka's doubles center on the theme of the two brothers or the two bureaucrats, whether one moves and the other remains immobile, or whether both move with the same movements.[1] It is no less true that the duos and trios interpenetrate. When one of the doubles remains immobile and is content to delegate movement to the other, it seems that this properly bureaucratic inertia has its origin in the familial triangle insofar as it keeps the child immobile and condemns him to reverie. In this respect, Kafka will say that the bureaucratic spirit is the social virtue that flows directly from familial education.[2] And, in the second case, where the doubles move together, their very activity supposes a third term such as an office director on whom they depend. It is in this way that Kafka constantly presents trios, formal bureaucratic triangulations. The two bureaucrats emanate necessarily from a superior third one, for whom they function as right arm and left arm. Inversely, then, if the bureaucratic double refers back to the familial triangle, the latter in turn can be replaced by bureaucratic triangles. And all these lines are very complicated in Kafka. Sometimes, with the familial triangle as a given, as in "The Metamorphosis," a term of another sort will come to be added or substituted: the chief clerk arrives behind Gregor's door and insinuates himself into the family. But sometimes, too, it is a trio of bureaucrats as a block that move in and take over the terms of the family, even if only provisionally: the introduction of the chief clerk in "The Metamorphosis" serves only to prepare for this moment. Sometimes, as in the beginning of *The Trial*, there isn't even a preexisting familial triangle (the father is dead, the mother is faraway), but there is still the intrusion of first one term and then another that function like policing doubles, and then their triangulation by a third term, the Inspector. We can observe the metamorphoses of this nonfamilial triangle that in turn will become the bureaucratic triangle of the bank employees, the apartment triangle of the voyeuristic neighbors, and the erotic triangle of Fraulein Burstner and her friends in a photo.

These complicated cases we've described have only a single goal—to show that for doubles as well as for triangles and for their mutual contacts and interpenetrations, something remains blocked. Why two or three and not more? Why does two refer to three and inversely? What stops another term, such as the sister in "The Metamorphosis," from doubling and triangulating in his or her own right? A failing of the letters in this respect, despite Kafka's attempt to introduce Grete Bloch and to escape from a duel-like relationship. A failing of the animalistic stories in this respect, despite Gregor's attempt to escape from triangulation. This is one of the main problems resolved by the novels: the doubles and the triangles that remain in Kafka's novels show up only at the beginning of the novels; and from the start, they are so vacillating, so supple and transformable, that they are ready to open onto series that break their form and explode their terms. This is the exact opposite of what happens in "The Metamorphosis," where the sister, as well as the brother, finds herself blocked by a triumphant return of the most exclusive sort of familial triangle. The question isn't deciding whether "The Metamorphosis" is a masterpiece. Obviously it is, but that doesn't help Kafka, since as much as it tells things so well, it prevents him, or so he believes, from writing a novel. He would never have stood for writing a familial or conjugal novel, a Saga of the Kafkas, or a Wedding Night in the Country. Yet already in *Amerika*, he had seen how proliferating series might be a solution; in *The Trial* and then in *The Castle*, he has a complete grasp of this solution. But from now on, there will be no reason for a novel to end. (Unless he does as Balzac, as Flaubert, as Dickens do; but however strong his admiration for them, he doesn't want any of that. He doesn't want to create a genealogy, even if it is a social one, à la Balzac; he doesn't want to erect an ivory tower, à la Flaubert; he doesn't want "blocks," à la Dickens, since he himself has a very different conception of the block. The only one that he will take as his master is Kleist, and Kleist also detested masters; but Kleist is a different matter even in the deep influence that he had on Kafka. We have to speak differently about this influence. Kleist's question isn't, "What is a minor literature and, further, a political and collective literature?" but rather, "What is a literature of war?" This is not completely alien to Kafka, but it is not exactly his question.)

By making triangles transform until they become unlimited, by proliferating doubles until they become indefinite, Kafka opens up a field of immanence that will function as a dismantling, an analysis, a prognostics of social forces and currents, of the forces that in his epoch are only beginning to knock on the door (literature has a sense only if the machine of expression precedes and anticipates contents). And, to a certain degree, it is no longer even necessary to make use of doubles and triangles; a central figure will start proliferating directly — for example, Klamm or, even more so, K himself. Thus, the terms tend to distribute themselves along a line of escape, to take flight on this line, in relation to the contiguous segments — police segment, lawyer segment, judge segment, ecclesiastical segment. At the same time that they lose their double or triangular form, these terms don't appear or don't appear only as the hierarchized representatives of the law but become agents, connective cogs of an assemblage of justice, each cog corresponding to a position of desire, all the cogs and all the positions communicating with each other through successive continuities. Exemplary in this respect is the scene of the first interrogation in which the tribunal loses its triangular form, with the judge at the top and the sides that split into a left side and a right side and realign along a single, continuous line that not merely reunites the two parties but prolongs them by bringing together "oafish Inspectors and Examining Magistrates . . . but also . . . a judicial hierarchy of high, indeed of the highest rank, with an indispensable and numerous retinue of servants, clerks, police, and other assistants, perhaps even hangmen." And after this first interrogation, the contiguity of offices comes increasingly to replace the hierarchy of triangles. All the functionaries are "venal," "corrupt." Everything is desire, the whole line is desire, both in those who dispose of a power and repress and in those who are accused and undergo power and repression (for example, the accused man, Block: "The man ceased to be a client and became the lawyer's dog"). One would be quite wrong to understand desire here as a desire *for* power, a desire to repress or be repressed, a sadistic desire and a masochistic desire. Kafka's idea has nothing to do with this. There isn't a desire for power; it is power itself that is desire. Not a desire-lack, but desire as a plenitude, exercise, and functioning, even in the most subaltern of workers. Being an assemblage, desire is precisely one with the gears and the components of the machine, one with the power of the machine. And the desire that someone has for power is only his fascination for these gears, his desire to make certain of these gears go into operation, to be himself one of these gears—or, for want of anything better, to be the material treated by these gears, a material that is a gear in its own way.

If I am not the typist, I am at least the paper that the keys strike. If I am no longer the machine's mechanic, I am least the living material with which it deals. Maybe this is a much more essential place, one that is closer to the gears than is the mechanic (for example, the subaltern officer of the Colony or the accused people in *The Trial*). The question is thus much more complicated than simply a question about two abstract desires, a desire to repress and a desire to be repressed, which could be put abstractly as a sadistic question and a masochistic one. Repression, for both the represser and the repressed, flows from this or that assemblage of power-desire, from this or that state of the machine—since there is also a need for mechanics as well as materials working in a strange harmony, in a connection more than in a hierarchy. Repression depends on the machine, and not the other way around. Thus, there isn't power as if it were an infinite transcendence in relation to the slaves or the accused. Power is not pyramidal as the Law would have us believe; it is segmentary and linear, and it proceeds by means of contiguity, and not by height and farawayness (hence, the importance of the subalterns).[3] Each segment is power, *a* power as well as a figure of desire. Each segment is a machine or a piece of the machine, but the machine cannot be dismantled without each of its contiguous pieces forming a machine in turn, taking up more and more place. Take the example of bureaucracy, since it fascinates Kafka, since Kafka is himself a bureaucrat of the future, working in Insurance (and Felice takes care of dictating machines—segmentary meeting between two components). There isn't a desire *for* bureaucracy, to repress or to be repressed. There is a bureaucratic segment, with its sort of power, its personnel, its clients, its machines. Or rather, there are all sorts of segments, contiguous bureaus, as in Barnabas's experience. All the gears, which are in fact equivalent despite all appearances, and which constitute the bureaucracy as desire, that is, as an exercise of the assemblage itself. The divisions of oppressor and oppressed, repressors and repressed, flow out of each state of the machine, and not vice versa. This is a secondary consequence. The secret of *The Trial* is that K himself is also a lawyer, also a judge. Bureaucracy is desire, not an abstract desire, but a desire determined in this or that segment, by this or that state of the machine, at this or that moment (for example, the segmentary monarchy of the Hapsburgs) Bureaucracy as desire is at one with the functioning of a certain number of gears, the exercise of a certain number of powers that determine, as a function of the composition of the social field in which they are held, the engineers as well as the engineered.

Milena said of Kafka, "For him life was an absolutely different thing than what it represented to others. Money, the stock-market, investments, *a type-writer*, these were so many mysterious things to him . . . so many passionate enigmas that he admired with a moving naïveté because they were commercial."[4] Naïveté? Kafka had no admiration for simple technical machines, but he well knew that technical machines were only the indexes of a more complex assemblage that brings into coexistence engineers and parts, materials and machined personnel, executioners and victims, the powerful and the powerless, in a single, collective ensemble—oh desire, flowing out of itself and yet perfectly determined each and every time. In this sense, there is certainly a bureaucratic eros that is a segment of power and a position of desire. And a capitalist eros. And a fascist eros. All the segments communicate with each other through variable contiguities. Capitalist America, bureaucratic Russia, Nazi Germany—in fact, all the "diabolical powers of the future"—are knocking at the door of Kafka's moment with segmental and contiguous blows. Desire: machines that dismantle into gears, gears that make up a machine in turn. The suppleness of the segments, the displacement of the barriers. Desire is fundamentally polyvocal, and its polyvocality makes of it a single and unique desire that flows over everything. The equivocal women of *The Trial* don't stop making the judges, the lawyers, and the accused come in a single act of bliss. And the cry of Franz, the warder punished for his thefts, the cry that K hears in a lumber room contiguous to the hallway of his office at the bank, seems to "come from some martyred instrument" but it is also a cry of pleasure, not in a masochistic sense but because the suffering machine is a component of a bureaucratic machine that never stops creating its own bliss (*jouir de soi-même*).

There is no longer a revolutionary desire that would be opposed to power, to the machines of power. We noted the deliberate absence of social critique in Kafka. In *Amerika*, the most terrible work conditions don't inspire any critique in K but simply make him more afraid of being excluded from the hotel. Although familiar with the Czech socialist and anarchist movements, Kafka doesn't follow their path. Passing a worker's march, Kafka shows the same indifference as K in *Amerika*: "They rule the streets, and therefore think they rule the world. In fact, they are mistaken. Behind them already are the secretaries, officials, professional politicians, all the modern satraps for whom they are preparing the way to power." The Russian Revolution seems to Kafka to be the production of a new segment, rather than an overthrowing and a renewal. The expansion of the Russian revolution is an advance, a segmental push forward, an increase that doesn't occur without a violent flood. "[The flood of the] Revolution evaporates and leaves behind only the slime of a new bureaucracy. The chains of tormented mankind are made out of red tape." Between the Hapsburg bureaucracy and the new Soviet bureaucracy, there is no question of denying that there has been a change, there is a new piece in the machine, or rather, a piece has made up an entirely new machine. "[The Worker's Accident Insurance Institution] is a creation of the labor movement. It should therefore be filled with the radiant spirit of progress. But what happens? The Institution is a dark nest of bureaucrats, in which I function as the solitary display-Jew."[5] Of course, Kafka doesn't see himself as a sort of party. He doesn't even pretend to be revolutionary, whatever his socialist sympathies may be. He knows that all the lines link him to a literary machine of expression for which he is simultaneously the gears, the mechanic, the operator, and the victim. So how will he proceed in this bachelor machine that doesn't make use of, and can't make use of, social critique? How will he make a revolution? He will act on the German language such as it is in Czechoslavakia. Since it is a deterritorialized language in many ways, he will push the deterritorialization farther, not through intensities, reversals, and thickenings of the language but through a sobriety that makes language take flight on a straight line, anticipates or produces its segmentations. Expression must sweep up content; the same process must happen to form. The proliferation of series as they appear in *The Trial* plays this role. Since the history of the world is already established, not out of an eternal return but out of the pressure of always new and always harder segments, he will accelerate the speed of segmentalization, this speed of segmental production; he will precipitate segmented series, he will add to them. Since the collective and social machines bring about a massive deterritorialization of man, Kafka will take this process farther, to the point of an absolute molecular deterritorialization. Criticism is completely useless. It is more important to connect to the virtual movement that is already real even though it is not yet in existence (conformists and bureaucrats are always stopping the movement at this or that point). It is not a politics of pessimism, nor a literary caricature or a form of science fiction.

*This method of segmentary acceleration or proliferation connects the finite, the contiguous, the continuous, and the unlimited.* It has several advantages. America is in the process of toughening and spreading its capitalism; the decomposition of the Austrian Empire and the rise of Germany are preparing the way for fascism; the Russian Revolution has quickly produced a new and unanticipated bureaucracy; methods have led to new trials *(nouveau procès dans le processus)*; "anti-Semitism has spread to the working class," and so on. Capital-

ist desire, fascist desire, bureaucratic desire, Thanatos also—everything is bang-
ing at the door. Since one can't count on the official revolution to break the
precipitated conjunction of the segments, one will have to count on a literary machine that will anticipate the precipitations, that will overcome diabolical powers
before they become established. Americanism, fascism, bureaucracy—as Kafka
said, it is less a mirror than a *watch that is running fast.*[6] Since there is no way
to draw a firm distinction between the oppressors and the oppressed or between
the different sorts of desire, one has to seize all of them in an all-too-possible
future, hoping all the while that this act will also bring out lines of escape, pa-
rade lines, even if they are modest, even if they are hesitant, even if—and especially if—they are asignifying. A little bit like the animal that can only accord
with the movement that strikes him, push it farther still, in order to make it return to you, against you, and find a way out.

But, in fact, we have entered an entirely different realm than that of the
becoming-animal. It is true that the becoming-animal was already digging a way
out, but the becoming-animal was incapable of going wholeheartedly into it. It
is true that the becoming-animal was already bringing about an absolute deterritorialization, but only through an extreme slowness and only in one of its
poles. It allowed itself then to be recaptured, reterritorialized, retriangulated.
The becoming-animal remained a family affair. With the force of the series or
of the segments, we see something else, much more strange. The movement of
man's deterritorialization that is proper to great machines and that traverses socialism as well as capitalism will come into force at top speed along the entire
series. From then on, desire will function in two coexisting states: on the one
hand, it will be caught up in this or that segment, this or that office, this or that
machine or state of machine; it will be attached to this or that form of content,
crystallized in this or that form of expression (capitalist desire, fascist desire,
bureaucratic desire, and so on). On the other hand and at the same time, it will
take flight on the whole line, carried away by a freed expression, carrying away
deformed contents, reaching up to the unlimited realm of the field of immanence
or of justice, finding a way out, precisely a way out, in the discovery that
machines are only the concretions of historically determined desire and that desire doesn't cease to undo them, straightening its bent head (the struggle against
capitalism, fascism, bureaucracy—a struggle much stronger than if Kafka had
spent his time on a critique). These two coexistent states of desire are the two
states of the law. On the one hand, there is the paranoiac transcendental law that
never stops agitating a finite segment and making it into a completed object,
crystallizing all over the place. On the other hand, there is the immanent schizo-
law that functions like justice, an antilaw, a "procedure" that will dismantle all
the assemblages of the paranoiac law. Because, once again, this is what it is all
about—the discovery of assemblages of immanence and their dismantling. To
dismantle a machinic assemblage is to create and effectively take a line of escape

that the becoming-animal could neither take nor create. It is a completely different line. A completely different deterritorialization. Let no one say that this line is present only in spirit, as though writing isn't also a machine, as though it isn't also an act, even when it is independent of publication. As though the machine of writing isn't also a machine (no more superstructural than any other, no more ideological than any other), sometimes taken up by capitalist, fascist, or bureaucratic machines, sometimes tracing a modest revolutionary line. Let us note Kafka's constant idea: even with a solitary mechanic, the literary machine of expression is capable of anticipating or precipitating contents into conditions that, for better or for worse, concern an entire collectivity. Antilyricism—"grasp the world" to make it take flight; instead of fleeing it, caress it.[7]

These two states of desire or law can be found at several levels. We should emphasize the fact of these two coexistent states because we cannot say in advance, "This is a bad desire, that is a good desire." Desire is a mixture, a blend, to such a degree that bureaucratic or fascist pieces are still or already caught up in revolutionary agitation. It is only in motion that we can distinguish the "diabolism" of desire and its "immanence," since one lies deep in the other. Nothing preexists anything else. It is by the power of his noncritique that Kafka is so dangerous. We can simply say that there are two coexistent movements, each caught up in the other. One captures desire within great diabolical assemblages, sweeping along in almost the same movement servants and victims, chiefs and subalterns, and only bringing about a massive deterritorialization of man by also reterritorializing him, whether in an office, a prison, a cemetery (paranoiac law). The other movement makes desire take flight through all the assemblages, rub up against all the segments without settling down in any of them, and carry always farther the innocence of a power of deterritorialization that is the same thing as escape (the schizo-law). This is why Kafka's "heroes" have such a curious status in relation to large machines and to assemblages: although the officer of "The Colony" was in the machine, first as its mechanic and then as its victim, and although the characters in the novels belong to this or that state of the machine outside of which they lose all their existence, it seems that K and a certain number of other characters who double him are always in a sort of adjacency to the machine, always in contact with this or that segment, but also always repelled, always kept outside, moving too fast to really be "captured up." For example, K in *The Castle*: while it is true that desire has no preexisting criteria, his wild desire for the segmental castle doesn't prevent him from having an extrinsic position that makes him take flight on an adjacent line. Adjacency—that is the schizo-law. In the same way, Barnabas the messenger, one of K's doubles in *The Castle*, is a messenger only in a self-designated way and must be particularly quick to deliver a message even though the very same quickness excludes him from official service and its segmental weight. In the same way, the Student, one of K's doubles in *The Trial*, never stops misleading the official usher and takes his wife while the usher is delivering a message ("Back again at top speed and yet the student was here before me"). This coexistence of two states of movement, two states of desire, two states of law, doesn't signify hesitation but rather an immanent experimentation that will open up all the polyvocal elements of desire, in the absence of any transcendental criteria. Contact and contiguity are themselves an active and continuous line of escape.

This coexistence of two states appears clearly in the fragment of *The Trial* published under the title "A Dream." On the one hand, there is a rapid and joyous sliding movement or deterritorialization that makes everything adjacent even at the moment when the dreamer seems to have fallen into an abyss ("The paths there were very winding, ingeniously made and unpractical, but he glided along one of them as if on a rushing stream with unshaken poise and balance"). On the other hand, there are these pathways, these equally rapid segments that moment by moment bring about deadly reterritorializations of the dreamer (the mound in the distance — suddenly closer — the gravediggers — suddenly, the artist — the embarrassment of the artist — the artist's writing on the tomb — the dreamer who digs a hole in the ground — his fall). Undoubtedly, this text sheds some light on the false ending of *The Trial*, that deadly reterritorialization of K in a hard segment, a "loose boulder."

These two states of movement, of desire or of law, show up again in the example that we started with, photos and bent heads. Because the photo as a form of expression functioned well as an Oedipal reality, childhood memory, or promise of conjugality; it captured desire in an assemblage that neutralized it, reterritorialized it, and cut it off from all its connections. It marked the defeat of metamorphosis. Thus, the form of content that corresponded to it was the head that was bent as an index of submission, the gesture of one who is judged or even of one who judges. But in *The Trial*, we see a proliferating power of the photo, of the portrait, of the image. The proliferation starts at the beginning, with the photos in Fraulein Burstner's room — photos that have the power to metamorphose those who look at them (in *The Castle*, it's rather the people in the photo or the portrait who gain the power to metamorphose). From the photos of Fraulein Burstner, we move to the obscene images in the judge's book, then to the photos of Elsa that K shows to Leni (as Kafka did with his Weimar photos in his first encounter with Felice), then to the unlimited series of Titorelli's tableaux, about which one could say, à la Borges, that they contain so many differences from each other because they are absolutely identical.[8] In short, the portrait or the photo that marked a sort of artificial territoriality of desire now becomes a center for the perturbation of situations and characters, a connector that precipitates the movement of deterritorialization. An expression freed from its constricting form and bringing about a similar liberation of contents. In fact, the submission of the bent head connects to the movement of the head that straightens or that pushes forward — from the judges, whose backs curved against the ceiling tend to push Justice out of the picture, to the artist of "A Dream" who does not "bend down though he ha[s] to bend forward" in an effort to not walk on the grave mound. The proliferation of photos and heads opens up new series and explores uncharted regions that extend as far as the unlimited field of immanence.

# Chapter 7
# The Connectors

Certain series are composed of special terms. These terms are distributed throughout the ordinary series, at the end of one series or at the beginning of another, and so mark the manner in which they link, transform, or proliferate — the manner in which a segment adds on to another or is born out of another. These special series are thus composed of remarkable terms that play the role of connectors, since in each case they augment the connections of desire in the field of immanence. Thus the sort of young woman that obsesses Kafka and that K meets in *The Castle* as well as *The Trial*. It appears that these young women are attached to this or that segment: Elsa, the girlfriend of K before his arrest, is so linked to the banking segment that she knows nothing of the trial — so linked that K himself, in going to look for her, no longer thinks about the trial and dreams only of the bank; the washerwoman is linked to the segment of the subordinate functionaries, the bailiff, and the judge; Leni is linked to the segment of the lawyers. In *The Castle*, Frieda is linked to the segment about the secretaries and the functionaries; Olga to the segment about the servants. But the remarkable role that each of these women assumes in her respective series causes them together to constitute an extraordinary series that proliferates in its own way, that traverses and resonates through all the segments. Not only is each one at the turning point of several segments (thus Leni simultaneously caresses the lawyer, the accused man, Block, and K), but there is even more: each, from her point of view in this or that segment is in "contact," in "connection," in "contiguity," with the essential — that is, with the castle, with the trial, as ultimate powers of the continuous. (Olga says, "It is not only through the servants them-

63

selves that I have a connection with the Castle . . . Perhaps [my father] will forgive me, too, for accepting money from the servants and using it for our family.") Thus, each of these women can propose aid to K. In the desire that animates them, as in the desire that they incite, *they provide the deepest evidence of the identity of justice, of desire, and of the young woman or the young girl.* The young woman resembles justice: both are without principles. Pure chance, "it receives you when you come and dismisses you when you go." As a short proverb in the Castle's village says, "The decisions of the administration are as timid as young girls." K says to Jeremy who is running toward the functionaries' hotel, "Is it a sudden desire for Frieda that's seized you? I've got it as well, so we'll go together side by side." K can be denounced, sometimes as a lewd figure, sometimes as a cupid or interested figure, and that is the way justice works. One can put it best by saying that social investments are themselves erotic and, inversely, that the most erotic of desires brings about a fully political and social investment, engages with an entire social field. And the role of the young girl or young woman ends when she breaks a segment, makes it take flight, makes it flee the social field in which she is participating, makes it take flight on the unlimited line in the unlimited direction of desire. Through the tribunal door where the student is violating her, the washerwoman makes everything take flight—K, the judge, the audience, the session itself. Leni makes K flee from the room where the uncle, the lawyer, and the boss are speaking, but in taking flight, he gains more control over his trial. It is almost always a woman who finds the service door, that is, who reveals the contiguity of that which one had thought to be faraway and who restores or installs the power of the continuous. The priest in *The Trial* reproaches K about this: "You cast about too much for outside help, especially from women."

What, then, is this genre of women with dark, sad eyes? They have their necks bare, uncovered. They call you, they press against you, they sit on your knees, they take your hand, they caress you and are caressed by you, they kiss you and mark you with their teeth or, in contrast, are marked by yours, they violate you and let themselves be violated, sometimes they suffocate you and even beat you; they are tyrannic but they let you go or even make you go, they chase you and always send you off. Leni has webbed fingers like some sort of leftover from a becoming-animal. But women present an even more precise blend of things; they are part sister, part maid, part whore. They are anticonjugal and antifamilial. Already we can see this in the stories: the sister in "The Metamorphosis," who has become a lowly worker in a store, becomes a maid for Gregor-insect, prevents the mother and the father from coming into the room, and turns against Gregor only when he shows himself to be too attached to the portrait of the lady in fur (then, the sister lets herself be taken up again by the family at the same time as she decides Gregor's death). In "Description of a Struggle," it is a maid, Annette, who starts everything going. In "A Country

Doctor," the groom attacks Rosa, the young maid, much as the student in *The Trial* had attacked the washerwoman, and imprints on her cheeks his "two rows of teeth"—while a sister discovers a mortal wound in her brother's side. But there is an even greater development of these young women in the novels. In *Amerika*, it is a maid who violates K and brings about his exile as a first deterritorialization (there is a scene of suffocation that is fairly analogous to the suffocation Proust's narrator feels when he kisses Albertine). Then, there is a sort of coquettish sister, ambiguous and tyrannical, who catches K in various judo holds and who is at the center of the break with the uncle, the second deterritorialization of the hero (in *The Castle*, it is Frieda herself who, not out of simple jealousy but out of a judgment of the law, will directly cause the break by referring to a major infidelity of K's, because K preferred his "contacts" with Olga or with the Olga segment). *The Trial* and *The Castle* multiply these women who in various ways reunite the qualities of sister, maid, and whore. Olga, the prostitute of the castle's servants, and so on. Minor qualities of minor characters—part of the project of a literature that wants to be deliberately minor and draws its revolutionary force from that.

The three qualities correspond to three components of the line of escape as well as to three degrees of freedom: freedom of movement, freedom of the statement, freedom of desire. First, there are the sisters. Since they belong to the family, they have the greatest desire of making the familial machine take flight. "In the past, especially, the person I am in the company of my sisters has been entirely different from the person I am in the company of other people. Fearless, powerful, surprising, moved as I otherwise am only *when I write*."[1] (Kafka always defined literary creation as the creation of a desert world populated by his sisters where he would enjoy an infinite liberty of movement). Second, there are the maids, lowly employees, and so on. Already caught in a bureaucratic machine, they have the greatest desire of making it take flight. The sound of maids is neither signifying nor musical; it is that sound born of silence, which Kafka looked for everywhere, where the utterance is already part of a collective assemblage, a collective complaint, without a subject of enunciation that hides itself or deforms. A pure, moving material of expression. From this comes their quality as minor characters, all the more open to treatment by literary creation: "These silent underdogs do everything one supposes them to be doing . . . If I imagine that he is looking at me insolently, then he really is."[2] Third, there are the whores. Maybe for Kafka they are at the intersection of all the machines—familial, conjugal, bureaucratic—that they are all the more able to make take flight. The choking or erotic asthma that they cause doesn't come only from their pressure and their weight on their clients, which doesn't last a very long time, but from the fact that with them, one penetrates deeper along a line of escape, "farther than ever man had wandered before, a country so strange that not even the air had any thing in common with his native air, where one might die of strangeness, and yet whose enchantment was such that one could only go on and lose oneself further."[3] But none of these elements have any value by themselves; all three are needed at the same time, in the same character if possible, in order to form the strange combination that Kafka so dreams about. To take her for a maid, but also for a sister, and also for a whore.[4]

This combined formula, which has value only as an ensemble, is that of schizo-incest. Psychoanalysis, because it understands nothing, has always confused two sorts of incest: the sister is presented as a substitute for the mother, the maid as a derivative of the mother, the whore as a reaction-formation. The group of "sister-maid-whore" will be interpreted as a kind of masochistic detour but, since psychoanalysis also doesn't understand anything about masochism, we don't have to worry much about that either.

(A short parenthesis on masochism. Kafka shares nothing with masochism as it is described in books of psychoanalysis. The observations of psychiatry in the nineteenth and the beginning of the twentieth centuries give a much more correct clinical picture of masochism. Kafka thus could have something in common with the real cartography of masochism and with Sacher-Masoch, whose themes show up in many masochists, even when these themes are effaced in modern interpretations. We can cite at random: the pact with the devil, a masochistic "contract" that opposes the conjugal contract and works to wish it away; the admiration for, and necessity of, vampirish letters—sometimes the letters controlled by Masoch, sometimes the classified ads put in the newspapers, Masoch-Dracula; the becoming-animal, for example, in Masoch, the becoming-bear or fur that has nothing to do with the father or the mother; the interest in maids and whores; the agonizing reality of prison, which is explained not only by the fact that Masoch's father was a prison director but also because, as a child, Masoch saw prisoners and frequented prisons—he made himself a prisoner to acquire the maximum degree of farawayness or the excess of contiguity; historical investment—Masoch thought about writing the cycles and segments of a history of the world by emphasizing in his own way the long history of oppressions; the decisive political intention—Masoch, who had a Bohemian origin, was also connected to the same minorities of the Austrian empire as Kafka, a Czech Jew. The fascination of Masoch for the Jews in Poland, in Hungary. Maids and whores form part of these minorities, these class struggles, even if necessarily within the family and conjugality. Masoch, too, builds a minor literature that is his very life, a political literature of minorities. One might object that a masochist is not necessarily central to the Hapsburg empire at the moment of its great dissolution. Of course—but he always has the possibility to build a minority literature within his own language and to be all the more political in that activity; he finds means of expression based on his form of genius, through an archaic, symbolist, and stereotyped utilization of language or, on the contrary, through a sobriety that pulls from the language a pure complaint and provocation. It is true that masochism is not the only method. It is even a weak method. It is all the more interesting to compare masochists and Kafkians, noting their differences, noting their unequal utilizations of the name, but also noting the similarities of their respective projects.)

What is this combined sort of schizo-incest? It is opposed in numerous ways to a neurotic Oedipal incest. The Oedipal incest occurs, or imagines that it occurs, or is interpreted as if it occurs, as an incest with the mother, who is a territoriality, a reterritorialization. Schizo-incest takes place with the sister, who is not a substitute for the mother, but who is on the other side of the class struggle, the side of maids and whores, the incest of deterritorialization. Oedipal incest corresponds to the paranoiac transcendental law that prohibits it, and it works to transgress this law, directly if it can bear to do so, symbolically for want of anything better: demented father (Kronos, the most honest of fathers, as Kafka said); abusive mother; neurotic son—before becoming paranoiac in turn and before everything starts up again in the familial-conjugal triangle—since in fact such transgression is nothing but a simple means of reproduction. Schizo-incest corresponds, in contrast, to the immanent schizo-law and forms a line of escape instead of a circular reproduction, a progression instead of a transgression (problems with the sister are certainly better than problems with the mother as schizophrenics well know). Oedipal incest is connected to photos, to portraits, to childhood memories, a false childhood that never existed but that catches desire in the trap of representation, cuts it off from all connections, fixes it onto the mother to render it all the more puerile or spoiled, in order to have it support all the other, stronger interdictions and to prevent it from identifying itself as part of the social and political field. Schizo-incest, in contrast, is connected to sound, to the manner in which sound takes flight and in which memory-less childhood blocks introduce themselves in full vitality into the present to activate it, to precipitate it, to multiply its connections. Schizo-incest with a maximum of connection, a polyvocal extension, that uses as an intermediary maids and whores and the place that they occupy in the social series—in opposition to neurotic incest, defined by its suppression of connection, its single signifier, its holding of everything within the limits of the family, its neutralization of any sort of social or political field. The opposition appears clearly in "The Metamorphosis," between the woman with the covered neck, as she appears in the photo as an object of Oedipal incest, and the sister, with her neck uncovered, playing the violin, an object of schizo-incest (should one stick to the photo or grab onto the sister?).

We can well understand the connective function of these women at the beginning of *The Trial* where "a young woman with sparkling black eyes who was washing children's clothes in a tub" indicates "with her hand the open door of the next room" (the same type of linkage occurs in the first chapter of *The Castle*). The women have a multiple function. The women mark the start of a series or the opening of a segment that they belong to; they also mark its end, whether K abandons them or whether they abandon K, since he has gone elsewhere without their even knowing it. They thus function as a sort of signal that one approaches and moves away from. But, above all else, each has precipitated her own series, her segment in a castle or a trial, by eroticizing it; and the following segment will only begin or end, will only be precipitated, through the action of another young woman. Powers of deterritorialization, they nonetheless operate within a territory beyond which they will not pursue you. We also have to watch out for two false interpretations concerning them: one, in the style of Max Brod, would have their erotic quality be no more than the superficial sign of a paradox of faith, a sort of Abraham's sacrifice; the other, picked up by Wagenbach, recognizes the real erotic character but only to see in it a factor that delays K or turns him away from his goal.[5] If there is an attitude that resembles Abraham's, at most it is that of the American uncle who brings about K's abrupt sacrifice. And, undoubtedly, this attitude becomes clearer in *The Castle*, where it is Frieda who brings about the same sacrifice by reproaching K for his "infidelity." But this infidelity comes from the fact that K has already moved into another segment, marked by Olga, whose arrival Frieda caused at the same time that she caused the termination of her own segment. Thus, women don't function to detour or delay events at the trial or in the castle: they bring about the deterritorialization of K by making territories, which each one *marks* in her own way, rapidly come into play (Leni's "odor like pepper," Olga's household odor: the leftovers of the becoming-animal).

But schizo-incest is not complete without another element—a sort of homosexual effusion. There again, in opposition to an Oedipal homosexuality, this is a homosexuality of doubles, of brothers or of bureaucrats. The mark of this homosexuality shows up in the famous, tight clothes that Kafka so loved: Arthur and Jeremy, the two doubles in *The Castle* who frame the love of K and Frieda, come quickly forward "in tight fitting clothes"; the subaltern servants don't have uniforms but "clothes so close-fitting [that] a peasant or a handworker couldn't make use of them"; Barnabas's desire is mediated by the intense desire for tight clothing, and his sister, Olga, will make some for him. The two policemen at the beginning of *The Trial*, who observe Fraulein Burstner's photo, wear "a closely fitting black suit furnished with all sorts of pleats, pockets, buckles, and buttons, as well as a belt, like a tourist's outfit, and in consequence looks eminently practical, though one could not quite tell what actual purpose it serves." And these two policemen will be whipped by an executioner "sheathed in a sort of dark leather garment which left his throat and a good deal of his chest and the whole of his arm bare." Today still, these are the clothes of American sadomasochists, dressed in leather or rubber, with folds, buckles, piping, and so on. But it seems that bureaucratic or fraternal doubles themselves function as homosexual indexes only. Homosexual effusion has another finality that is no more than pointed to by these indexes. In "Memoirs of the Kalda Railroad," the narrator has a manifest homosexual relationship with the inspector ("We fell together in an embrace that often lasted ten hours unbroken"). But this relationship will find its real end only when the inspector is replaced by the artist. Some of the passages in *The Trial* on Titorelli will be deleted by Kafka because of their explicitness: "K remained on his knees before him . . . carressed his cheeks," and Titorelli pulls K along like a "light boat on the waves," initiating him into the secrets of the tribunal; the light changes direction and strikes him directly on his face "like a blinding cataract."[6] Similarly, in "A Dream," the artist breaks away from the two funereal bureaucratic doubles who come out of the bushes, "drawing figures in the air," entering with K into a relationship of tacit effusion.

Thus, the artist, too, functions as a remarkable element. The homosexual relationship with the artist is connected to the incestuous relationship with the young women or the little sisters (hence, the series of the perverse, voyeuristic girls who see or hear everything going on at Titorelli's and who start yelling when K takes off his vest, "He's taken off his jacket now"). But this is not the same sort of relationship. We have to distinguish three active elements: (1) the ordinary series, where each series corresponds to a determined segment of the machine and where the terms are constituted by proliferating bureaucratic doubles with all the marks of homosexuality (for example, the series of porters, the series of servants, the series of functionaries; note the proliferation of the Klamm's doubles in *The Castle*); (2) the remarkable series of young women, where each corresponds to a point that stands out from the ordinary series, whether at the opening of the segment, at its end point, or at a point of internal rupture, but always involved with an increase of valency and connection, a passage which precipitates into another segment (this is the function of eroticization or of schizo-incest); (3) the singular series of the artist, manifestly homosexual, which possesses the power of the continuous and which overflows all the segments and sweeps up all the connections. Whereas the young women ensure or "aid" K's deterritorialization by making him flee from segment to segment, the closest light always coming from behind him from a candle or a candelabra, the artist in contrast ensures a shifting and continuous line of flight where light comes from in front like a cataract. Whereas the young women are to be found at the principal points of connection for the pieces of the machine, the artist reunites all these points, arranges them in his own specific machine which extends across the whole field of immanence, and even anticipates it.

The points of connection between series or segments, the remarkable points and the singular points, seem in several respects to be asthetic impressions. They are often sensible qualities, odors, lights, sounds, contacts, or free figures of the imagination, elements from a dream or a nightmare. They are connected to chance. For example, in the fragment "The Substitute," three points of connection intervene: the portrait of the king, the little bit of the phrase that the anarchist is supposed to have pronounced ("Hey, you up there, bandit!), the popular song ("While the little lamp is burning"). They intervene to determine new couplings, and cause the proliferation of series; and the substitute notes that they can enter into innumerable polyvocal combinations, forming segments that are more or less near each other, more or less distant.[7] But it would be a great error to refer the points of connection to the aesthetic impressions that subsist in them. *Everything Kafka does works to an exactly opposite end*, and this is the principle behind his antilyricism, his anti-aestheticism: "Grasp the world," instead of extracting impressions from it; work with objects, characters, events, in reality, and not in impressions. Kill metaphor. Aesthetic impressions, sensations, or imaginings still exist for themselves in Kafka's first essays where a certain influence of the Prague school is at work. But all of Kafka's evolution will consist in effacing them to the benefit of a sobriety, a hyper-realism, a machinism that no longer makes use of them. This is why subjective impressions are systematically replaced by points of connection that function objectively as so many signals in a segmentation, so many special or singular points in a constitution of series. To speak here of a projection of phantasms would be to compound the error. These points coincide with the female characters or the artist characters, but all these characters exist only as objectively determined pieces and cogs of a machine of justice. The substitute knows quite well that the three elements can only find their connection and realize the ambiguity of their connection, the multiplicity of their connection, in a process that he engages in a perverse learning of. He is the veritable artist. A process or, as Kleist would say, a life-plan, a discipline, a method, not at all a phantasm. Titorelli himself, in the singularity of his position, is still part of the field of justice.[8] The artist is nothing like an aesthete, and the artist machine, the machine of expression, has nothing to do with artistic impressions. Moreover, insofar as such impressions can still be found to operate in female or artistic connections, the artist himself is only a dream. The formula of the artist machine or of the machine of expression must be defined in a completely different way, then, not only independently of any aesthetic intention but also beyond the female characters and the artist characters who intervene objectively in the series or at the limit of the series.

In fact, these connector characters, with their connotations of desire, incest, or homosexuality, receive their objective nature from the machine of expression, and not the other way around: these are contents drawn along by the machine of expression, and not the other way around. No one knew better than Kafka to define art or expression without any sort of reference to the aesthetic. If we try to sum up the nature of the artistic machine for Kafka, we must say that it is a bachelor machine, the only bachelor machine, and, as such, plugged all the more into a social field with multiple connections.[9] Machinic definition, and not an aesthetic one. The bachelor is a state of desire much larger and more intense than incestuous desire and homosexual desire. Undoubtedly, it has its problems, its weaknesses, such as its moments of lowered intensity: bureaucratic mediocrity, going around in circles, fear, the Oedipal temptation to lead the hermit's life ("[H]e can live only as a hermit or a parasite"), and, even worse, the suicidal desire for self-abolition ("His nature is suicidal, therefore, he has teeth only for his own flesh and flesh only for his own teeth"). But, even with these downfalls, it is a production of intensities ("The bachelor has only the moment"). He is the deterritorialized, the one who has neither "center" nor "any great complex of possessions": "[H]e has only as much ground as his two feet take up, only as much of a hold as his two hands encompass, so much the less, therefore, than the trapeze artist in a variety show, who still has a safety net hung up for him below." His trips aren't those of the bourgeoisie on an ocean-liner, "with much effect, roundabout," a package tour, but the schizo-voyage, "on a few planks of wood that even bump against and submerge each other." His voyage is a line of escape, like a "weathervane on a mountain." And, undoubtedly, this flight takes place in place, in a pure intensity ("He lay down, as children now and then lie down in the snow in winter in order to freeze to death"). But even in place, the flight doesn't consist in fleeing the world, in taking refuge in the tower or in the phantasm or in impression — flight can alone keep "him on the tips of his toes and *only the tips of his toes could have kept him on the earth.*" There is nothing less aesthetic than the bachelor in his mediocrity, but there is nothing more artistic. He doesn't flee the world; he grasps it and makes it take flight on a continuous and artistic line: "I must just take my walks and that must be sufficient, but in compensation there is no place in all the world where I could not take my walks." With no family, no conjugality, the bachelor is all the more social, social-dangerous, social-traitor, a collective in himself ("We are outside the law, no one knows it and yet everyone treats us accordingly"). This is the secret of the bachelor: his production of intensive quantities — the lowest as in "little dirty letters," the highest as in the unlimited *oeuvre* He produces this production of intensive quantities directly on the social body, in the social field itself. A single, unified process. The highest desire desires both to be alone and to be connected to all the machines of desire. A machine that is all the more social and collective insofar as it is solitary, a bachelor, and that, tracing the line of escape, is equivalent in itself to a community whose conditions haven't yet been established. Such is the objective definition of the machine of expression, which, as we have seen, corresponds to the real state of a minor literature where there is no longer any "individual concern." Production of intensive quantities in the social body, proliferation and precipitation of series, polyvalent and collective connections brought about by the bachelor agent — there is no other definition possible for a minor literature.

# Chapter 8
# Blocks, Series, Intensities

Everything that we've said about the contiguous and the continuous in Kafka may seem contradicted, or in any case attenuated, by the role and importance of discontinuous blocks. The theme of blocks is constant in Kafka and seems affected by an insurmountable discontinuity. There has been a lot of discussion of Kafka's broken form of writing, of his mode of expression through fragments. "The Great Wall of China" is precisely the form of content that corresponds to this expression: scarcely have the workers finished one block then they are sent far away to do another, leaving gaps everywhere that may never be filled in. Can we say that this discontinuity is the distinctive feature of the short stories? There is something deeper at work. Discontinuity imposes itself on Kafka especially when there is representation of a transcendental, abstract, and reified machine. In this sense, the infinite, the limited, and the discontinuous are similar. Each time that power presents itself as a transcendental authority, as a paranoid law of the despot, it imposes a discontinuous distribution of individual periods, with breaks between each one, a discontinuous repartition of blocks, with spaces between each one. In fact, the transcendental law can only regulate pieces that revolve around it at a distance from it and from each other. It is an astronomical construction. It is the formula for ostensible acquittal in *The Trial*. And that's what "The Great Wall of China" makes clear: the emperor's council wanted the fragmentary style for the wall; and the fragments refer so much to the imperial transcendence and a hidden unity that certain persons feel that the discontinuous wall will find its only finality in a tower ("First the wall . . . then the tower").

Kafka will not renounce this principle of discontinuous blocks or distant frag-

72

ments turning around an unknown transcendental law. And why would he renounce it, since it is a state of things, even if superficial (and what is as-
tronomy?), and since this state functions well in his work. But we must connect
it to constructions of another sort, which correspond to the discovery that the
novels make, where K becomes increasingly aware that the transcendental imperial law refers in fact to an immanent justice, to an immanent assemblage of
justice. Paranoid law gives way to a schizo-law; immediate resolution gives way
to an unlimited deferral; the transcendence of duty in the social field gives way
to a nomadic immanence of desire that wanders all over this field. This is made
explicit in "The Great Wall of China," without being developed in any way: there
are nomads who give evidence of another law, another assemblage, and who
sweep away everything in their journey from the frontier to the capitol, the emperor and his guards having taken refuge behind the windows and the screens.
Thus, Kafka no longer operates by means of infinite-limited-discontinuous but
by finite-contiguous-continuous-unlimited. (Continuity will always seem to him
to be the condition of writing, not only for writing the novels but also for writing
the short stories such as "The Verdict." The unfinished work is no longer a fragmentary work but an unlimited one).[1]

What happens from the point of view of the continuous? Kafka doesn't abandon the blocks. But we might begin by saying that these blocks, instead of dis-
tributing themselves around a circle in which only several discontinuous arches
are traced, align themselves on a hallway or a corridor: each one thereby forms
a segment, which is more or less distant, on this unlimited straight line. But that
doesn't yet bring about a sufficient change. Since they persist, it is the blocks
themselves that have to change their form, at the very least by moving from one
point of view to another. And, in fact, if it is true that each block-segment has
an opening or a door onto the line of the hallway—one that is usually quite far
from the door or the opening of the following block—it is also true that all the
blocks have back doors that are contiguous. This is the most striking topography
in Kafka's work, and it isn't only a "mental" topography: two diametrically opposed points bizarrely reveal themselves to be in contact. This situation shows
up constantly in *The Trial*, where K, opening the door of a tiny room close to
his office at the bank, finds himself in the judicial site where the two inspectors
are being punished; going to see Titorelli "in a suburb which was almost at the
diametrically opposite end of the town from the offices of the court," he notices
that the door at the back of the painter's room leads into precisely the same judicial site. It's the same in *Amerika* and *The Castle*. Two blocks on a continuous
and unlimited line, with their doors far from each other, are revealed to have
contiguous back doors that make the blocks themselves contiguous. And even
here we're simplifying things: the hallway can be angled, the little door can be
connected to the line of the hallway, in such a way that things become all the
more surprising. The line of the hallway, the unlimited straight line, can hold

other surprises, since it can connect to a certain degree with the principle of the discontinuous circle and the tower (as in the villa in *Amerika* or in the Castle, which includes a tower as well as a group of small, contiguous buildings).

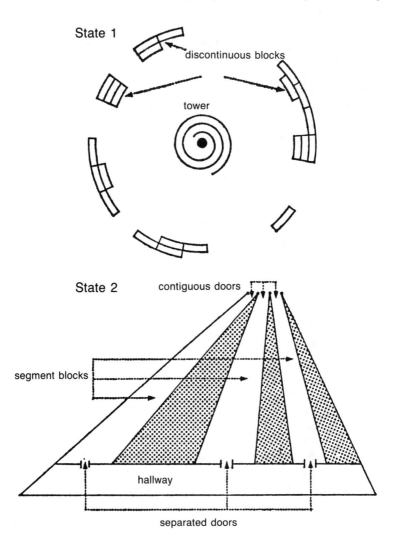

Let's try to briefly outline these two architectural states:

| State 1 | State 2 |
|---|---|
| High-angle or low-angle | Frontal view, corridor view |
| Stairs | Low ceiling |
| Craning up, craning down | Wide-angle and depth-of-field |
| Discontinuity of block-arches | Unlimitedlessness of the |
|  | immanent hallway |
| Astronomical model | Earthly or underground model |
| Distant and close | Faraway and contiguous |

Note 1: We want to emphasize that there is simultaneously a real distinction between the two states of architecture and the possibility of their interpenetration. They are distinct because they correspond to two different bureaucracies — the old and the new; the old, imperial, despotic, Chinese bureaucracy, the new capitalist or socialist bureaucracy. They penetrate because the new bureaucracy doesn't easily bring about new forms: not only do many people "believe" in the old bureaucracy (the notion of belief in Kafka), but this bureaucracy is not a mere covering over the new one. The modern bureaucracy is born naturally out of the old forms which it reactivates and changes by giving them a completely contemporary form. This is why the two states of architecture have an essential coexistence, which Kafka outlines in the majority of his texts: the two states function in each other, and in the modern world. Levels in a celestial hierarchy *and* contiguity of virtually underground offices. Kafka himself is at the border of the two bureaucracies: the insurance company and then the worker's insurance office where he works take care of the business of advanced capitalism, but they contain the archaic and already outmoded structure of an older capitalism and an older bureaucracy. More generally, it is difficult to believe that Kafka, always attentive to the 1917 revolution, would not have heard at the end of his life about the avant-garde and constructivist projects in Russia. Tatlin's project for the Third International was presented in 1920: a spiral tower with four rotating rooms, each turning at different speeds according to an astronomical model (the legislative branch, the executive branch, and so on). Moholy-Nagy's project was presented in 1922 in Hungary: people would become "a part of the function of the tower" which included an external ramp with a guard-rail, an interior and unprotected spiral called the "athlete's path," an elevator, and a large motor. A paranoiac avant-garde. It seems that the most modern functionalism more or less voluntarily reactivated the most archaic or mythical forms. Then, too, there is a mutual penetration of two bureaucracies, that of the past and that of the future (we're still at this stage today). Realizing this mixture, we can only distinguish the following as the two poles *archaisms with a contemporary function* and *neoformations*. It seems to us that Kafka was one of the first

to recognize this historical problem, at least as well as did some of his more "engaged" contemporaries such as the Constructivists and the Futurists. For example, Khlebnikov invents two languages; one can ask to what degree they can rejoin each other, to what degree they differ from each other: the astronomical, algorithmic, stellar language of pure logic and high formalism, and the underground "zaoum" that works with a pure asignifying material, insensity, sonority, contiguity. It is as though there were two remarkable bureaucratic styles, each pushed to its extreme—that is, each following its own line of escape. Even though his situation is quite different, Kafka's problem is the same and also concerns language, architecture, bureaucracy, lines of escape.

Note 2: To note the degree to which the two states are mixed we need to cite in detail the example of the castle. For the castle itself keeps many of the structures that correspond to the first state (height, the tower, hierarchy). But these structures are constantly modified or effaced to the profit of the second state (arrangement and contiguity of offices with moving boundaries). And, above all else, the inn for gentlemen from the castle brings about the triumph of the second state, with its long hallway and its contiguous and dirty rooms where the functionaries work in bed.

Note 3: All this can explain the interest of Orson Welles for Kafka. Cinema has a much greater link than theater with architecture (Fritz Lang, architect). But Welles always brought together two architectural models and consciously used them. The first model is that of splendors and decadence, of archaisms, but possessing a completely contemporary function, rise and descent along infinite stairways, low-angle and high-angle shots. The second model is that of the wide-angle and depth-of-field, unending hallways, contiguous traversals. *Citizen Kane* and *The Magnificent Ambersons* use the first model whereas *The Lady from Shanghai* uses the second. Even though *The Third Man* isn't credited to Welles, it reunites the two models in an astonishing mixture of the sort that we've been talking about: archaic stairways, the great ferris-wheel sticking up into the sky, the rhizome-sewers that are barely underground, the contiguity of the sewer pipes. Always the infinite paranoiac spiral and the unlimited schizoid line. The film of *The Trial* is even better at combining the two movements; and a scene like that of Titorelli—the little girls, the long hallway in wood, long shots, and sudden contiguities—shows the affinity of Welles's genius with Kafka.

Note 4: Why have we aligned *the faraway and the contiguous* (the second state), on the one hand, with *the distant and the close* (the first state), on the other? It has nothing to do with the words; we could have chosen others: it is a question of experimentation and concepts. In the architectural figures of the great wall and the tower, it is true that the blocks that form arches of the circle are close to each other—they join up by forming couples. It is also true that they remain distant from each other, since gaps that will never be filled remain between them. Furthermore, the transcendental law, the infinite tower, is infinitely distant from each block; and, at the same time, it is always very close and never ceases to send its messager to each block, bringing one near the other when it moves away from the other, and so on. The infinitely distant law emits hypostases, sends emanations that always come closer and closer. Sometimes distant, sometimes close, it is the formula for the periods or successive phases of superficial acquittal. Simultaneously distant and close, it is the formula for the law that rules these periods and these phases (isn't the great paranoiac always on our case and yet infinitely distanced from us?). The text from "The Great Wall of China," "An Imperial Message," sums up this situation: the emperor is close to each of us and sends us his emanation but he is no less the All Distant One, since the messenger will never arrive—too many places to cross, too many things in the way, themselves distant from each other. However, on the other side, there is *faraway and contiguous*. Faraway is opposed to close, contiguous is opposed to distant. But in the grouping of experiences and concepts, faraway is equally opposed to distant, contiguous opposed to close. In fact, the offices are very far from each other because of the length of the hallway that separates them (they aren't very close), but they are contiguous because of the back doors that connect them along the same line (they aren't very distant). The essential text in this respect would be the short aphorism where Kafka says that the contiguous village is at the same time so faraway that it would take a lifetime to reach it. Kafkaesque problem: must we "believe" that this text says the same thing as the imperial messenger? Shouldn't we believe rather that it says the exact opposite? Because close and distant belong to the same dimension—height—dominated by the axis of a movement that traces the figure of a circle where a point distances itself from others and approaches them. But contiguous and faraway belong to another dimension—length—the rectilinear straight line, transversal to the trajectory of movement, that brings into contiguity the most separated segments. To put this more concretely, we could say that the mother and the father, as in "The Metamorphosis," are close and distant: they are emanations of the law. But the sister is not close: she is contiguous—contiguous and faraway. Or take the case of bureaucracy: the bureaucratic Other is always contiguous—contiguous and faraway.

The two functioning architectural groups thus take shape in the following way: on the one hand, infinite-limited-discontinuous-close and distant; on the other hand, unlimited-continuous-finite-faraway and contiguous. Yet, in both cases, Kafka proceeds by blocks. Blocks—the thing and the word show up all the time in the Diaries, sometimes to designate unities of expression, sometimes to designate unities of content, and sometimes to mark a flaw, sometimes to mark a virtue. For example, virtue consists in "preserving all [my] powers in [a block]."[2] But the problem is that there are also blocks that are artificial or stereotypical. Kafka finds Dickens's work, which he very much admires and takes as the model for *Amerika*, to have this quality. His admiration is tempered by his estimation of the ways blocks are constituted in Dickens: "These rude characterizations which are artificially stamped on everyone and without which Dickens would not be able to get on with his story even for a moment."[3] In Kafka's work, we can see how the blocks change their nature and function, tending toward a utilization that is increasingly sober and polished. First of all, there are the blocks that correspond to the fragmentary construction of the Great Wall of China: separated blocks that are distributed in discontinuous arches of the circle *(block-arches)*. In a second situation, the blocks are well determined segments that are already aligned on an unlimited straight line, but with variable intervals: this is the composition in *Amerika*, from the point of view of expression, as well as that of contents, the villa, the hotel, the theater *(block-segments)*. But *The Trial* brings a new perfection to the method: the contiguity of the offices. The segments on the unlimited straight line become contiguous, even though they are quite separated from each other; they also lose their exact boundaries to the benefit of moving frontiers that shift and come together with them in a continuous segmentation *(block-series)*. Without a doubt, this topographical perfection is taken to its highest degree in *The Trial*, even more so than in *The Castle*. But, inversely, *The Castle* brings about another sort of progress by breaking away from that which was too spatial in *The Trial* in order to bring out what was already there but still too covered up by spatial figures: the series become intensive, the journey reveals itself as an intensity, the map is a map of intensities, and the moving frontiers are themselves thresholds *(blocks of intensity)*. The whole first chapter of *The Castle* works in this mode, from threshold to threshold, from low intensities to high ones and vice versa, part of a cartography that is certainly not interior or subjective but that has definitely ceased to be spatial. The low intensity of the bent head, the high intensity of the head that straightens and the sound that takes flight, a passage from one scene to another by thresholds: a language that has become intense makes its contents take flight in place on this new map.

This implies a certain method, both a procedure *(procédure)* of expression and an operation *(procédé)* of content. This method was already present in *Amerika* and in *The Trial*. But it now emerges with a specific force and gives to the blocks their fifth and final sense — as *childhood blocks*. Kafka's memory was never very good; but that's all the better, since the childhood memory is incurably Oedipal and prevents desire and blocks it onto a photo, bends the head of desire and cuts it off from all its connections (" 'Oh well, memories,' said I. 'Yes, even remembering in itself is sad, yet how much more like its object!' ").[4] Memory brings about a reterritorialization of childhood. But the childhood block functions differently. It is the only real life of the child; it is deterritorializing; it shifts in time, with time, in order to reactivate desire and make its connections proliferate; it is intensive and, even in its lowest intensities, it launches a high intensity. Incest with the sister and homosexual activity with the artist are examples of such childhood blocks (as the little girl blocks at Titorelli's already demonstrate). The first chapter of *The Castle* brings a childhood block into operation in an exemplary manner when K, at a moment of lowered intensity (his deception in front of the Castle), relaunches or reactivates the whole structure by injecting into the castle tower the deterritorializing bell of his native land. To be sure, children don't live as our adult memories would have us believe, nor as their own memories, which are almost simultaneous with their actions, would have them believe. Memory yells "Father! Mother!" but the childhood block is elsewhere, in the highest intensities that the child constructs with his sisters, his pal, his projects and his toys, and all the nonparental figures through which he deterritorializes his parents every chance he gets. Ah, childhood sexuality – it's certainly not Freud who gives us the best sense of what that is. The child doesn't cease reterritorializing everything back onto his parents (the photo); he has need of lowered intensities. But in his activity, as in his passions, he is simultaneously the most deterritorialized and the most deterritorializing figure – the Orphan.[5] He also forms a block of deterritorialization that shifts with time, the straight line of time, coming to reanimate the adult as one animates a puppet and giving the adult living connections.

Not only as realities but as method and discipline, the childhood blocks never stop shifting in time, injecting the child into the adult, or the superficial adult into the real child. Yet in Kafka and in his work, this transport produces a very strange mannerism. This is not the symbolic and allegorical mannerism of the Prague school. This is not the mannerism of those who play at being a child, that is, who imitate the child or represent him. It is a mannerism of sobriety without memory, where the adult is captured up in a childhood block without ceasing to be an adult, just as the child can be caught up in an adult block without ceasing to be a child. This is not an artificial exchange of roles. Rather, it is the strict contiguity of two faraway segments. It's a little like what we saw with the becoming-animal: a becoming-child of the adult taking place in the adult, a becoming-adult of the child taking place in the child, the two in contiguity. *The Castle* presents these intensive mannerist scenes well: in the first chapter, the men bathe and "roll about in the bath," while the children watch and are "driven back by mighty splashes"; and inversely, little Hans, the child of the woman in black, "is [impelled] chiefly [by] some such boyish fancy. The seriousness he evinced in everything he did seemed to indicate it" – as adult as only a child can be (a reference to the bathing scene shows up here). But, already in *The Trial*, there is a great mannerist scene: when the warders are all punished, the whole sequence is treated as a childhood block; each line shows that these are children who are getting whipped and who are crying out, even if they are only half serious. It seems in this respect that children, according to Kafka, go farther than women: they form a block of transport and of deterritorialization that is much more intense than the female series; they are caught up in a mannerism that is much stronger and an assemblage that is much more machinic (for example, the little girls around Titorelli; and in "Temptation in the Village," the connection to the woman and to the children have different degrees of complexity). We still have to refer to another mannerism in Kafka—a sort of worldly mannerism: the "horrible politeness" of the two gentlemen in *The Trial* who come to execute K and to whom K replies by putting on his new gloves; and, then, the manner by which they move their butcher knife over K's body. The two mannerisms have complementary and opposed functions: the mannerism of politeness tends to separate that which is contiguous (Stay back! A bow, a too studied salute, an overly insistent submission—this can be a way of saying "Shit" to the authorities). The mannerism of childhood works in an inverse way. But, together, the two mannerisms, the two poles of mannerism, constitute Kafka's schizo-buffoonery. Schizophrenics are well acquainted with both mannerisms; that's their way of deterritorializing social coordinates. It is probable that Kafka made ample use of them in his life as well as in his work: the machinic art of the marionette (Kafka often talks about his personal mannerisms—the tightening of the jaw that almost leads to catatonia).[6]

# Chapter 9
# What Is an Assemblage?

An assemblage, the perfect object for the novel, has two sides: it is a collective assemblage of enunciation; it is a machinic assemblage of desire. Not only is Kafka the first to dismantle these two sides, but the combination that he makes of them is a sort of signature that all readers will necessarily recognize. Take, for example, the first chapter of *Amerika*, published separately as "The Stoker." The chapter considers the boiler room as a machine: K constantly declares his intention to be an engineer or at least a mechanic. But if the boiler room isn't described in itself (and, anyway, the boat is in port), that is because a machine is never simply technical. Quite the contrary, it is technical only as a social machine, taking men and women into its gears, or, rather, having men and women as part of its gears along with things, structures, metals, materials. Even more, Kafka doesn't think only about the conditions of alienated, mechanized labor — he knows all about that in great, intimate detail — but his genius is that he considers men and women to be part of the machine not only in their work but even more so in their adjacent activities, in their leisure, in their loves, in their protestations, in their indignations, and so on. The mechanic is a part of the machine, not only as a mechanic but also when he ceases to be one. The stoker is part of the "room of machines," even, and especially, when he pursues Lina who has come from the kitchen. The machine is not social unless it breaks into all its connective elements, which in turn become machines. The machine of justice is a machine metaphorically: this machine fixes the initial sense of things, not only with its rooms, its offices, its books, its symbols, its topography, but also with its personnel (judges, lawyers, bailiffs), its women who are adjacent to the porno books of the law, its accused figures who make up an interdeterminate material. A writing machine exists only in an office. The office exists only with its secretaries, its section heads, and its bosses; its social, political, and administrative distribution; and also its erotic distribution without which there would never have been any "technics." This is so because the machine is desire – but not because desire is desire of the machine but because desire never stops making a machine in the machine and creates a new gear alongside the preceding gear, indefinitely, even if the gears seem to be in opposition or seem to be functioning in a discordant fashion. That which makes a machine, to be precise, are connections, all the connections that operate the disassembly.

That the technical machine is only a piece in a social assemblage that it presupposes and that alone deserves to be called machinic introduces another point: the machinic assemblage of desire is also the collective assemblage of enunciation. This is why the first chapter of *Amerika* is filled with the protestations of the German stoker who complains about his immediate superior, a Rumanian, and about the oppression that the Germans undergo on the boat. The statement *(enoncé)* may be one of submission, or of protestation, or of revolt, and so on; but it is always part of the machine. The statement is always juridical, that is, it always follows rules, since it constitutes the real instructions for the machine. This is not to say that differences in the statements don't matter; quite the contrary, it matters a great deal to know if it is a revolt or a petition (Kafka will say that he is astonished by the docility of injured workers: "They come to us and beg. Instead of storming the institute and smashing it to little pieces, they come and beg"[1] But whether petition, revolt, or submission, the statement always undoes an assemblage of which the machine is a part; it is itself part of the machine that will form a machine in turn in order to make possible the functioning of the whole or to modify it or to blow it up. In *The Trial*, a woman asks K: Is it reforms that you want to introduce? In *The Castle*, K situates himself immediately in a combative relation to the castle (and, in a variant version, the combat appears even more explicitly). But, in any case, there are rules that tell how to take things apart and from which one can't really tell if submission doesn't finally conceal the greatest sort of revolt and if combat doesn't imply the worst of acceptances. In the three novels, K appears in an astonishing mixture: he is an engineer or a mechanic who deals with the gears of the machine; he is a jurist or a legal investigator who follows the statements of the assemblage (K has to speak only for his uncle, who has never seen him, to recognize him: "You are my own dear nephew. I suspected it all the time"). There is no machinic assemblage that is not a social assemblage of desire, no social assemblage of desire that is not a collective assemblage of enunciation.

Kafka himself is at the border. Not only is he at the turning point between two bureaucracies, the old and the new, but he is between the technical machine and the juridical statement. He has experienced their reunion in a single assemblage. In the insurance company, he deals with industrial accidents, the degree of safety of various types of machinery, boss-worker conflicts, and related declarations.[2] And certainly, in Kafka's work, it is not only a question of technical machines in themselves or of the juridical statement in itself; rather, the technical machine furnishes the model of a form of content that is applicable to the whole social field, whereas the juridical statement furnishes the model for a form of expression applicable to any statement. What is essential in Kafka is that machine, statement, and desire form part of one and the same assemblage that gives the novel its unlimited motor force and its objects. It is shocking to see Kafka assimilated by certain critics to the literature of the past even if they allow that he used this literature to construct a sort of Summation, a universal Bibliography, a total Oeuvre based on the force of fragments. This is too French a view of Kafka. No more than Don Quixote does Kafka remain in the world of books. His ideal library would include only texts for engineers or machinists or jurists (plus several authors that he admires for their genius, and also for secret reasons). His literature is not a voyage through the past but one through our future. Two problems enthrall Kafka: *when can one say that a statement is new?* – for better or for worse – *and when can one say that a new assemblage is coming into view?* – diabolical or innocent, or both at the same time. An example of the first problem: when the beggar of "The Great Wall of China" brings a manifesto written by the revolutionaries of the adjoining province, the signs utilized "have for us an archaic character" that make us say, "Ancient history told long ago, old sorrows long since healed." An example of the second: the diabolical powers of the future that are already knocking at the door – capitalism, Stalinism, fascism. It is that which Kafka listens to, and not the noise of books – the sound of a contiguous future, the murmer *(rumeur)* of new assemblages of desire, of machines, and of statements, that insert themselves into the old assemblages and break with them.

In what sense is the statement always collective even when it seems to be emitted by a solitary singularity like that of the artist? The answer is that the statement never refers back to a subject. Nor does it refer back to a double – that is, to two subjects, one of which would act as the cause or the subject of enunciation and the other as a function or the subject of the statement. There isn't a subject who emits the statement or a subject about which the statement would be emitted. It is true that the linguists who make use of this complementarity define it in a more complex way by considering "the marking of the process of enunciation in the enounced statement" (as in terms like *I, you, here, now*). But in whatever way this relation is conceived, we don't believe that the statement can be connected to a subject, doubled or not, divided or not, reflected or not. Let's return to the problem of the production of new statements and to so-called minor literature, since this literature, as we have seen, is in an exemplary situation for the production of new statements. When a statement is produced by a bachelor or an artistic singularity, it occurs necessarily as a function of a national, political, and social community, even if the objective conditions of this community are not yet given to the moment except in literary enunciation. From this arises two principle theses in Kafka: literature as a watch that moves forward and literature as a concern of the people. The most individual enunciation is a particular case of collective enunciation. This is even a definition: an statement is literary when it is "taken up" by a bachelor who precedes the collective conditions of enunciation. This is not to say that this collectivity that is not yet constituted (for better or for worse) will in turn become the true subject of enunciation or even that it will become the subject that one speaks about in the statement: in either case, that would be to fall into a sort of science fiction. No more than the bachelor, the collectivity is not a subject of enunciation or the statement. But the actual bachelor and the virtual community—both of them real—are the components of a collective assemblage. And it is not enough to say that the assemblage produces the statement as a subject would; it is in itself an assemblage of enunciation in a process that leaves no assignable place to any sort of subject but that allows us all the more to mark the nature and the function of the statements, since these exist only as the gears and parts of the assemblage (not as effects or products).

This is why it is useless to ask who K is. Is he the same in the three novels? Is he different in each novel? At the limit, one could say that in his letters, Kafka makes complete use of the double, of the appearance of two subjects, one of enunciation and the other of the statement—but he makes use of them only for a game and a bizarre undertaking, adding the greatest ambiguity to their opposition, having no aim other than to blur the distinction and make them exchange their respective roles. In the stories, it is already the assemblage that takes the place of all subjects. But either it is a transcendental, reified machine that keeps the form of a transcendental subject or it is a becoming-animal that already has suppressed the problem of the subject but that does no more than point ahead to the assemblage or it is a molecular becoming-collective that the animal indicates but that still seems to function as a collective subject (the mice people, the dog people). In his passion for writing, Kafka explicitly conceives of the stories as a counterpart of the letters, as a means to disavow the letters and the persistent trap of subjectivity. But the stories are imperfect in this respect, simple stopping points or breathing spaces. It is with the novels that Kafka reaches the final and really unlimited solution: K will not be a subject but will be a general function that proliferates and that doesn't cease to segment and to spread over all the segments. We still have to specify each of these points. On the one hand, general is not opposed to individual; general designates a function, and the most solitary individual has a function that is all the more general in that it connects to all the terms of the series through which it passes. In *The Trial*, K is a banker and, through this segment, is in connection with a whole series of functionaries, clients, and his girlfriend, Elsa; but he is also arrested and connected to the inspectors, the witnesses, and Fraulein Burstner; and he is accused and connected to the bailiffs, the judges, and the washerwoman; and he is, in litigation, connected to the lawyers and to Leni; and he is an artist, connected to Titorelli and the little girls. The general function is inseparably social and erotic—the functional is simultaneously the functionary and desire. On the other hand, it is true that doubles continue to play a large role in each of these series of the general function, but they do so as points of departure or as a final homage to the problem of the two subjects; the question of the double is surpassed; and K proliferates without needing to double himself or to make use of doubles. Ultimately, it is less a question of K as a general function taken up by an individual than of K as a *functioning of a polyvalent assemblage of which the solitary individual is only a part*, the coming collectivity being another part, another piece of the machine—without our knowing yet what this assemblage will be: fascist? revolutionary? socialist? capitalist? Or even all of these at the same time, connected in the most repugnant or diabolical way? We don't know, but we have ideas about all of these—Kafka taught us to have them.

Why, from this point on, in the assemblage of desire, does the juridical aspect of the enunciation take over the machinic aspect of the enunciation or of the thing itself? Or, if it doesn't take it over, it at least precedes it. The respect for forms in Kafka, the extraordinary respect of the three K's for the great totalities of America, for the already Stalinist apparatus of justice, for the already fascist machine of the castle, show no submission but only the exigencies and necessities of a rule of enunciation. It is in this way that Kafka makes use of the law. The enunciation precedes the statement, not as the function of the subject that would have produced it but as a function of an assemblage that makes this into its first gear in order to connect to other gears that will follow and that will be installed as time goes by. In each series of *The Castle* or of *The Trial*, one can find an enunciation, even if rapid or allusive, that is especially asignifying and yet that is immanent to the whole series: in the first chapter of *The Castle*, a peasant's or teacher's phrase or gesture doesn't form statements, but only enunciations that play the role of connectors. This primacy of the enunciation refers us once again to the conditions of minor literature: it is the expression that precedes or advances—it is expression that precedes contents, whether to prefigure the rigid forms into which contents will flow or to make them take flight along lines of escape or transformation. But this primacy doesn't imply any idealism. Because the expressions or the enunciations are no less strictly determined by the assemblage than are the contents themselves. And it is one and the same desire, one and the same assemblage, that presents itself as a machinic assemblage of content and as a collective assemblage of enunciation.

The assemblage doesn't have two sides only. On the one hand, it is segmental, extending itself over several contiguous segments or dividing into segments that become assemblages in turn. This segmentalization can be more or less rigid or supple. But suppleness can be as constraining and more crushing than rigidity, as in *The Castle* where the contiguous offices seem to have movable barriers between them, a fact that renders even more unbearable all of Barnabas's ambition: always another office after the office that one has entered into, always another Klamm behind the Klamm that one has already met. The segments are simultaneously powers and territories—they capture desire by territorializing it, fixing it in place, photographing it, pinning it up as a picture, or dressing it in tight clothes, giving it a mission, extracting from it an image of transcendence to which it devotes itself to such a degree that it comes to oppose this image to itself. In this sense, we have seen how each block-segment was a concretization of power, of desire, of territoriality or reterritorialization, regulated by the abstraction of a transcendental law. But we must declare as well that an assemblage has points of deterritorialization; or that it always has a line of escape by which it escapes itself and makes its enunciations or its expressions take flight and disarticulate, no less than its contents that deform or metamorphose; or that the assemblage extends over or penetrates *an unlimited field of immanence* that makes the segments melt and that liberates desire from all its concretizations and abstractions or, at the very least, fights actively against them in order to dissolve them. These three things are in fact the same thing: the field of justice against the transcendental law, the continuous line of escape against the segmentalization of the blocks, the two great points of deterritorialization, one turning the expressions into a sound that takes flight or into a language of intensities (against the photos), the other taking the contents "head over heels and away" (against the bent head of desire). The fact that immanent justice, the continuous line, points, or singularities are active and creative becomes evident in the way they assemble *(s'agencent)* and form a machine in turn. This always takes place as part of collective conditions, although minor, the conditions of minor literature and politics, even if each of us had to discover in himself or herself an intimate minority, an intimate desert (we must note the dangers of a minority struggle—to reterritorialize, to redo the photos, to remake power and law, to also remake a "great literature").

Thus far we have opposed the abstract machine to concrete machinic assemblages. The abstract machine is that of the colony, or of Odradek or Blumfeld's ping-pong balls. Transcendent and reified, seized by symbolical or allegorical exegeses, it opposes the real assemblages that are worth nothing except in themselves and that operate in an unlimited field of immanence—a field of justice as against the construction of the law. But, from another point of view, it would be necessary to reverse this relationship. In another sense of abstract (a sense that is nonfigurative, nonsignifying, nonsegmental), it is the abstract machine that operates in the field of unlimited immanence and that now mixes with it in the process or the movement of desire: the concrete assemblages are no longer that which gives a real existence to the abstract machine by taking away its transcendental pretense; it's almost the reverse now—it's the abstract machine that measures the mode of existence and the reality of the assemblages in terms of the capacity that they demonstrate for undoing their own segments, for pushing farther their points of deterritorialization, for taking flight on the line of escape, for filling the field of immanence. The abstract machine is the unlimited social field, but it is also the body of desire, and it is also Kafka's continuous oeuvre in which intensities are produced and in which are inscribed all sorts of connections and polyvalences. Let us cite at random some of Kafka's assemblages (we don't pretend to be making an exhaustive list, since some group several others together or are themselves parts of others): the assemblage of letters, the machine for making letters; the assemblage of the becoming-animal, the animalistic machines; the assemblage of the becoming-female or the becoming-child, the mannerisms of female blocks or childhood blocks; the large assemblages that deal with commercial machines, hotel machines, bank machines, judiciary machines, bureaucratic machines, and so on; the bachelor assemblage or the artistic machine of the minority. We can use several criteria to judge their degree and mode, even in the smallest details.

First, to what degree can this or that assemblage do without the mechanism of transcendental law? The less it can do without it, the less it is a real assemblage; the more it is an abstract machine in the first sense of the word, the more it is despotic. For example, can the familial assemblage do without a triangulation, can the conjugal assemblage do without a doubling, that make of them legal hypostases rather than functional assemblages? Second, what is the nature of the segmentalization proper to each assemblage? More or less hard or supple in the delimitation of its segments, more or less rapid or slow in their proliferation? The more the segments are hard or slow, the less the assemblage is capable of effectively fleeing and following its own line of escape or its points of deterritorialization, even if this line is strong and these points are intense. In this case, the assemblage functions only as an indication rather than as a real, concrete assemblage: it doesn't succeed in bringing itself into full effect—that is, in rejoining the field of immanence. And whatever the escapes that it indicates, it is condemned to defeat and allows itself to be captured by the preceding mechanism. For example, the defeat of the becoming-animal especially in "The Metamorphosis" (reconstitution of the familial block). The becoming-female seems much richer in suppleness and proliferation, and the becoming-child, Titorelli's little children, is even more so. The childhood blocks or the childish mannerisms in Kafka seem to have a function of escape or deterritorialization that is more intense than that of the female series. Third, taking into account the nature of its segmentalization and the speed of its segmentations, what is the ability of an assemblage to overflow its own segments—that is, to spread over the line of escape and expand over the field of immanence? An assemblage can have a supple and proliferating segmentalizaton, and yet be oppressive and exercise a power that is great, especially since it is not even despotic any more but, rather, really machinic. Instead of flowing into the field of immanence, it segments this field in its own way. The false ending of *The Trial* even brings about a typical sort of retriangulation. But, independent of this ending, what is the ability of the Trial assemblage, of the castle assemblage, to open onto a whole field of unlimited immanence that blurs all the segmentary offices and doesn't take place as a punctual ending but is already at work in each limit and at every moment? Only under these conditions will it no longer be an abstract machine (abstract in a primary, transcendental sense) that is realized only in the assemblage but, rather, will become the assemblage that moves toward the abstract machine (in a secondary and immanent sense). And fourth, what is the ability of a literary machine, an assemblage of enunciation or expression, to form itself into this abstract machine insofar as it is a field of desire? The conditions of a minor literature? To quantify Kafka's work would be to play on these four criteria, these intensive quantities, to produce all the corresponding intensities from the lowest to the highest: the K function. But that is just what he did, that is precisely his continuous oeuvre.

Notes

# Notes

## FOREWORD. THE KAFKA EFFECT

1. Walter Benjamin, "Franz Kafka," in *Illuminations*, translated by Harry Zohn, edited and introduced by Hannah Arendt (New York: Schocken Books, 1969), p. 127. The following passages from Benjamin's essay will be taken from this edition; page references will appear in the text.

2. I am referring here to the concept that the Marrocan writer Abdelkebir Khatibi introduces in his book, *Amour Bilingue* (Paris: Fata Morgana, 1984).

3. Gilles Deleuze and Claire Parnet, *Dialogues* (Paris: Flammarion, Collection Dialogues, 1977), pp. 125–26; see also the important chapter entitled "De la supériorité de la littérature anglaise-américaine," pp. 47–63.

4. See Roland Barthes, *Sade, Fourier, Loyola*, trans. Richard Miller (New York: Hill and Wang, 1976).

5. Gilles Deleuze and Félix Guattari, *Mille Plateaux* (Paris: Minuit, 1980), p. 166.

6. I am referring to the excellent book by Sarah Kofman, *Mélancolie de l'art* (Paris: Editions Galilée, 1985), pp. 26–27.

7. In a letter cited in the very fine article that Irving Wohlfarth devoted to Benjamin in the *Revue d'Esthétique*, new series, no. 1 (Paris: Ed. Privat, 1981). The article is entitled "Sur quelques motifs juifs chez Benjamin." The extract from the letter that I am using here is found in note 18, p. 161. Wohlfarth recalls that Gershom Scholem recommended to Benjamin that he "begin every study on Kafka with the book of Job or at least with a discussion about the possibility of divine judgment": Scholem considered divine judgment to be the "only subject of Kafka's work"!

8. See p. 122. Maurice de Gandillac, in his translation of Benjamin's text on Kafka ("Kafka," in *Poésie et Révolution*, 2 [Paris: Editions Denoël]), tells us that in the Talmudic tradition the Halakah is an oral law of which not a single word can be changed; the Haggadah is a free interpretation.

9. For further reference to these problems, see Wohlfarth's text that I mentioned in note 7, and the following articles that appear in the same issue of the *Revue d'Esthétique*: Jürgen Habermas, "L'actualité de Walter Benjamin. La critique: prise de conscience ou préservation," pp. 107–31, and Yves Kobry, "Benjamin et le langage," pp. 171–79.

## CHAPER 1. CONTENT AND EXPRESSION

1. The naked or covered female neck has as much importance as the bent or straightened male head: "the neck encircled by black velour," "the collerette in silk lace," "the collar of fine white silk," and so on.

2. Already, we can find it in a 20 December 1902 letter to a childhood friend, Oskar Pollak: "[W]hen Shamefaced Lacky stood up from his stool his big angular head went right through the ceiling, and without his particularly wanting to he had to look down on the thatched roofs" (Franz Kafka, *Letters to Friends, Family and Editors*, trans. Richard and Clara Winston [New York: Schocken Books, 1977], 6). And in a diary entry for 1913: "To be pulled in through the ground-floor window of a house by a rope tied around one's neck" (*The Diaries of Franz Kafka*, trans. Joseph Kresh [New Youk: Schocken Books, 1948], 1:191).

3. "Description of a Struggle," in Franz Kafka, *Complete Stories* (New York: Schocken Books, 1971), 39. (The first part of "Description of a Struggle" continually develops this double movement of bent head–straightened head and the connections of the latter to sounds.)

4. Multiple apparitions of the cry in Kafka's work: crying in order to be heard crying—the death cry of a man enclosed in a room—"[I] screamed aloud, to hear only my own scream which met no answer nor anything that could draw its force away, so that it rose up without check and could not stop even when it ceased being audible" ("Unhappiness," in Kafka, *Complete Stories*, 390–91).

5. For example, Marthe Robert doesn't simply propose a psychoanalytic Oedipal interpretation of Kafka; she wants the portraits and the photos to serve as *trompe-l'oeil* images, the sense of which can be painfully deciphered. She also wants bent heads to signify impossibles quests. (*Oeuvres complètes*, Cercle du livre precieux, 3:380).

6. "A Report to an Academy," in Kafka, *Complete Stories*, 259.

## CHAPTER 2. AN EXAGGERATED OEDIPUS

1. Max Brod, *Franz Kafka: A Biography* (New York: Schocken Books, 1960), 20: "Kafka knew these [Freudian] theories very well and considered them always as a very rough and ready explanation which didn't do justice to detail, or rather to the real heartbeat of the conflict." (Nonetheless, Brod seems to think that the Oedipal experience does apply to the child and only later finds itself reworked as a function of the experience of God; pp. 32–33). In a letter to Brod (Kafka, *Letters*, November 1917, 167), Kafka says about a particular book of psychoanalysis that, "[I]t shares the quality of other psychoanalytic works that in the first moments its thesis seems remarkably satisfying, but very soon after one feels the same old hunger."

2. Gustave Janouch, *Conversations with Kafka* (London: Andre Deutsch, 1971), 68.

3. Kafka, *Diaries*, 24 January 1922, 210.

4. Theodore Herzl, quoted by Wagenbach, *Franz Kafka, Années de jeunesse* (Paris: Mercure, 1967), 69.

5. Letter to Brod, in Wagenbach, *Franz Kafka*, 156: "Diabolical powers, whatever their message might be, brush up against the doors and rejoice already from the fact that they will arrive soon."

6. Note, for example, Kafka's enduring disdain for Zionism (as a spiritual and physical reterritorialization): Wagenbach, *Franz Kafka*, 164–67.

7. Kafka, *Diaries*, 29 January 1922, trans. Martin Greenberg (New York: Schocken Books, 1949), 2:215.

8. There is another version of the same text where it is a question of a sanitarium: compare, the ape's cough.

## CHAPTER 3. WHAT IS A MINOR LITERATURE?

1. See letter to Brod, Kafka, *Letters*, June 1921, 289, and commentaries in Wagenbach, *Franz Kafka*, 84.

2. Kafka, *Diaries*, 25 December 1911, 194.

3. Ibid., 193: "[L]iterature is less a concern of literary history, than of the people."

4. See "Wedding Preparations in the Country", in Kafka, *Complete Stories*: "And so long as you say 'one' instead of 'I,' there's nothing in it" (p. 53). And the two subjects appear several pages later: "I don't even need to go to the country myself, it isn't necessary. I'll send my clothed body," while the narrator stays in bed like a bug or a beetle (p. 55). No doubt, this is one of the origins of Gregor's becoming-beetle in "The Metamorphosis" (in the same way, Kafka will give up going to meet Felice and will prefer to stay in bed). But in "The Metamorphosis," the animal takes on all the value of a true becoming and no longer has any of the stagnancy of a subject of enunciation.

5. See Michel Ragon, *Histoire de la littérature prolétarienne en France* (Paris: Albin Michel, 1974) on the difficulty of criteria and on the need to use a concept of a "secondary zone literature."

6. Kafka, *Diaries*, 25 December 1911, 193: "A small nation's memory is not smaller than the memory of a large one and so can digest the existing material more thoroughly."

7. See the excellent chapter "Prague at the turn of the century," in Wagenbach, *Franz Kafka*, on the situation of the German language in Czechoslavakia and on the Prague school.

8. Constancy of the theme of teeth in Kafka. A grandfather-butcher; a streetwise education at the butcher-shop; Felice's jaws; the refusal to eat meat except when he sleeps with Felice in Marienbad. See Michel Cournot's article, "Toi qui as de si grandes dents," *Nouvel Observateur*, April 17, 1972. This is one of the most beautiful texts on Kafka. One can find a similar opposition between eating and speaking in Lewis Carroll, and a comparable escape into non-sense.

9. Franz Kafka, *The Trial*, trans. Willa and Edwin Muir (New York: Schocken Books, 1956): "[H]e noticed that they were talking to him, but he could not make out what they were saying, he heard nothing but the din that filled the whole place, through which a shrill unchanging note like that of a siren seemed to sing."

10. Kafka, *Diaries* 20 August 1911, 61–62.

11. Kafka, *Diaries*: "Without gaining a sense, the phrase 'end of the month' held a terrible secret for me" especially since it was repeated every month—Kafka himself suggests that if this expression remained shorn of sense, this was due to laziness and "weakened curiosity." A negative explication invoking lack or powerlessness, as taken by Wagenbach. It is well-known that Kafka makes this sort of negative suggestion to present or to hide the objects of his passion.

12. Kafka, *Letters to Milena*, 58. Kafka's fascination with proper names, beginning with those that he invented: see Kafka, *Diaries*, 11 February 1913 (à propos of the names in *The Verdict*).

13. Kafka commentators are at their worst in their interpretations in this respect when they regulate everything through metaphors; thus, Marthe Robert reminds us that the Jews are *like* dogs or, to take another example, that "since the artist is treated as someone starving to death Kafka makes him into a hunger artist; or since he is treated as a parasite, Kafka makes him into an enormous insect" (*Oeuvres complètes*, Cercle du livre precieux, 5:311). It seems to us that this is a simplistic conception of the literary machine—Robbe-Grillet has insisted on the destruction of all metaphors in Kafka.

14. See, for example, the letter to Pollak in Kafka, *Letters*, 4 February 1902, 1–2.

15. See H. Vidal Sephiha, "Introduction à l'étude de l'intensif," in *Langages* 18 (June 1970): 104–20. We take the term *tensor* from J.-F. Lyotard who uses it to indicate the connection of intensity and libido.

16. Sephiha, "Introduction," 107 ("We can imagine that any phrase conveying a negative notion of pain, evil, fear, violence can cast off the notion in order to retain no more than its limit-value — that is, its intensive value": for example, the German word *sehr*, which comes from the Middle High German word, *Ser* meaning "painful").

17. Wagenbach, *Franz Kafka*, 78–88 (especially 78, 81, 88).

18. Kafka, *Diaries*, 15 December 1910, 33.

19. Henri Gobard, "De la vehicularité de la langue anglaise," *Langues modernes* (January 1972) (and *L'Alienation linguistique: analyse tetraglossique*, [Paris: Flammarion, 1976]).

20. Michel Foucault insists on the importance of the distribution between what can be said in a language at a certain moment and what cannot be said (even if it can be *done*). Georges Devereux (cited by H. Gobard) analyzes the case of the young Mohave Indians who speak about sexuality with great ease in their vernacular language but who are incapable of doing so in that vehicular language that English constitutes for them; and this is so not only because the English instructor exercises a repressive function, but also because there is a problem of languages (see *Essais d'ethnopsychiatrie générale* [Paris: Gallimard, 1970], 125–26).

21. On the Prague Circle and its role in linguistics, see *Change*, No. 3 (1969) and 10 (1972). (It is true that the Prague circle was only formed in 1925. But in 1920, Jakobson came to Prague where there was already a Czech movement directed by Mathesius and connected with Anton Marty who had taught in the German university system. From 1902 to 1905, Kafka followed the courses given by Marty, a disciple of Brentano, and participated in Brentanoist meetings.)

22. On Kafka's connections to Lowy and Yiddish theater, see Brod, *Franz Kafka*, 110–16, and Wagenbach, *Franz Kafka*, 163–67. In this mime theater, there must have been many bent heads and straightened heads.

23. "An Introductory Talk on the Yiddish Language," trans. Ernst Kaiser and Eithne Wilkins in Franz Kafka, *Dearest Father* (New York: Schocken Books, 1954), 381–86.

24. A magazine editor will declare that Kafka's prose has "the air of the cleanliness of a child who takes care of himself" (see Wagenbach, *Franz Kafka*, 82).

25. "The Great Swimmer" is undoubtedly one of the most Beckett-like of Kafka's texts: "I have to well admit that I am in my own country and that, in spite of all my efforts, I don't understand a word of the language that you are speaking."

## CHAPTER 4. THE COMPONENTS OF EXPRESSION

1. Kafka, *Diaries*, 15 December 1910, 33.

2. Gustave Janouch, *Conversations*, 143 (and p. 158: "Form is not the expression of the content but only its power of attraction").

3. Letter to Brod, Kafka, *Letters*, 13 July 1912, 80.

4. We are making use here of an unpublished study by Claire Parnet on *The Vampire and Letters* where the Kafka-Dracula connection is specifically analyzed. See also all the texts that Elias Canetti cites in *The Other Trial: Kafka's Letters to Felice* (New York: Schocken Books, 1974); but in spite of these texts, Canetti doesn't seem to notice this vampirish activity and speaks instead about Kafka's shame over his body, his humiliation, his distress, and his need for protection.

5. See the admirable text in Kafka, *Letters to Milena*, 228–31. Dictating or typing machines fascinated Kafka in every possible way — bureaucratically, commercially, erotically. Felice worked in a business that sold "parlographs" and she became the firm's manager. Kafka was seized by a fever of advice and propositions about ways to get parlographs into hotels, post offices, trains, ships, and zeppelins and to combine them with typewriters, with "praxinoscopes," with the telephone. Kafka was obviously enchanted and thought that in this way he could console Felice who wanted to cry: "I sacrifice my nights to your business. Answer me in detail." Kafka, *Letters to Felice*, 166–68. With

a great commercial and technical elan, Kafka wants to introduce the series of diabolical inventions into the nice series of beneficial inventions.

6. Kafka, *Letters to Felice*, 17 November, 1912, 47.

7. Kafka, *Diaries*, 19 January 1911, 43.

8. "Devilish in my innocence": see Kafka, *Diaries*, 65. And in "The Judgment," the father says, "An innocent child, yes, that you were, truly, but still more truly have you been a devilish human being! — And therefore take note: I sentence you now to death by drowning!"

9. Proust's letters are above all else topographies of social, psychical, physical and geographic obstacles; and the obstacles are much larger the closer the correspondent is to them. This is obvious in the letters to Madame Strauss, which, like the letters to Milena, have a certain Angel of Death quality to them. In Proust's letters to young men, there are even more topographical obstacles relating to space and time, means, states of the soul, conditions, changes. For example, in a letter to a young man, where it seems that Proust no longer wants him to come to Cabourg, "You are free to decide what you want, and if you decide to come, don't write, but telegraph me right away when you arrive and, if possible take a train that arrives around 6 in the evening, or at least toward the end of the afternoon or after dinner but not too late and not before two in the afternoon, since I would like to see you before you've seen anyone. But I'll explain all of that if you come."

10. On the prison, see Kafka *Diaries*, 19 January 1911, 43.

11. Bachelard, *Lautreamont* (Paris: Editions Corti, 1956); for discussion of pure action, speed, and attack as characteristics of Lautreamont and the slowness of Kafka understood as a wearing down of "the will to live," see Bachelard's first chapter.

12. Kafka often contrasts two types of voyage, an extensive and organized one, and one that is intense, in pieces, a sinking or fragmentation. This second voyage takes place in a single place, in "one's bedroom," and is all the more intense for that: "Now you lie against this, now against that wall, so that the window keeps moving around you . . . I must just take my walks and that must be sufficient, but in compensation there is no place in all the world where I could not take my walks." (Kafka, *Diaries*, 19 July 1910, 27-28.) An intensive America, a map of intensities.

13. Kafka, *Diaries*, 9 February 1915, 2:115.

14. Kafka, *Diaries*, 8 August 1917, 2:179.

15. Kafka, *Letters to Felice*, 17 November 1912, 47.

16. The anger of Kafka when he is treated as a writer of intimacy: hence, from the start of his letters to Felice, his violent reaction against readers or critics who speak above all else of his interior life. In France, indeed, the initial success of Kafka was based on this misunderstanding — a Kafka who is simultaneously intimate and symbolical, allegorical and absurd. This is discussed in Marthe Robert's excellent study on the conditions of the reading of Kafka in France, "Citoyen de l'utopie" in *Les Critiques de notre temps et Kafka* (Paris:Garnier 1973). We can say that Kafka studies really began when German and Czech critics noted the importance of his belonging to a strong bureaucracy (insurance company, social security) and his attraction to the socialist and anarchist movements in Prague (something he often hid from Max Brod). Wagenbach's two books translated into French, *Kafka par lui-même* (Paris: Editions du Seuil, 1968) and *Franz Kafka, Années de jeunesse*, are essential references for all these questions.

Another aspect is the role of the comic and the joyful in Kafka. But this is the same thing: the politics of the statement *(énoncé)* and the joy of desire. Even if Kafka is sick or dying, even if he brandishes guilt as his own private circus, to repel whatever bores him. It is not coincidental that every interpreter fascinated by neurosis insists simultaneously on a tragic or anguished side of Kafka and on an apolitical side. Kafka's gaiety, or the gaiety of what he wrote, is no less important than its political reality and its political scope. The best part of Max Brod's book on Kafka is when Brod tells how listeners laughed at the reading of the first chapter of *The Trial* "quite immoderately" (p. 178). We don't see any other criteria for genius than the following: the politics that runs through it and the joy that it communicates. We will term "low" or "neurotic" any reading that turns genius into anguish, into tragedy, into a "personal concern." For example, Nietzsche, Kafka, Beckett, whomever: those who don't read them with many involuntary laughs and political tremors are deforming everything.

In these components of Kafka's work—letters, stories, novels—we haven't dealt with two elements: on the one hand, very short texts, somber aphorisms, and relatively pious parables, as in the breakup with Felice in 1918 when Kafka is really sad, tired, and thus incapable of writing and lacking a desire to write. On the other hand, we haven't dealt with the *Diaries* for an inverse reason. Namely, that the *Diaries* touch upon everything: it is the rhizome itself. It is not an element in the sense of one aspect of the work, but the element (in the sense of milieu) that Kafka declares he never wants to leave, just like a fish. This is so because this element communicates with all of the outside and distributes the desire of the letters, the desire of the stories, the desire of the novels.

## CHAPTER 5. IMMANENCE AND DESIRE

1. See Herman Uyttersprot, *Eine neue Ordnung der Werke Kafkas?* (Antwerp: Vries-Brouwers, 1957).

2. Kafka, *The Trial*, 127: "Above all, if he were to achieve anything, it was essential that he should banish from his mind once and for all the idea of possible guilt. This legal action was nothing more than a business deal such as he had often concluded to the advantage of the Bank, a deal within which, as always happened, lurked dangers which must simply be obviated."

3. Petit-bourgeois intimacy and the absence of any sort of social criticism will be the primary themes in the opposition of the communists to Kafka. Take the example of the study done by the weekly journal *Action* in 1946: "Faut-il brûler Kafka?" [Should we burn Kafka?] Then, things get even tougher and Kafka will be increasingly denounced as an active antisocialist who engages in a struggle against the proletariat by means of the portrait that he paints of bureaucracy. Sartre intervened in the Moscow Peace Conference in 1962 to call for a better analysis of the connections between art and politics and of Kakfa in particular. Then followed two colloquia in Liblice in Czechoslavakia (1963 and 1965) dealing with Kafka. The participants saw there signs of a deep change; and, in fact, there were important presentations by Golsdtucker, Fischer, and Karst. But there were no Russian participants, and the presentations had little resonance in the socialist literary press. The East German press was the only one to talk about it, but only to denounce it. These conferences and the influence of Kafka were then attacked as one of the causes of the spring revolts in Prague. Golsdtucker declared that "we have been accused, Ernst Fischer and myself, of having wanted to eliminate Goethe's Faust, symbol of the working class, from the spirit of socialists in order to replace him by Kafka's sad hero, Gregor Samsa, man metamorphosed into a bug." Golsdtucker had to emigrate to England, and Karst to America. On all these points, on the respective position of the different Eastern governments, and on Karst and Golsdtucker's recent statements, see the excellent article by Antonin Liehm, "Kafka dix ans apres," *Les Temps modernes* (July 1973).

4. Kafka, *The Trial*, 40: "You may object that it is not a trial at all; you are quite right, for it is only a trial if I recognize it as such."

5. It seems to us to be completely wrong to define the unlimited delay as a state of "trouble," "indecision," "guilty conscience."

## CHAPTER 6. PROLIFERATION OF SERIES

1. The two cases often show up in Kafka: the two that make the same movement together—for example, the appearance of Arthur and Jeremy in the first chapter of *The Castle*; the immobile double who sends his double to move around; see the theme of "The Man Who Disappeared," "The Judgment," and, in *The Castle*, Sortini and Sordini ("[Sordini] exploits the resemblance in name to push things on Sortini's shoulders, especially any duties falling on him as a deputy, so that he can be left

undisturbed to his work"). It seems that the first case is only a preparation for the second: even Arthur and Jeremy separate, Arthur returning to the Castle while Jeremy moves around the town and loses his youthfulness. On the bureaucratic quality of the double, see one of Dostoevsky's masterpieces, *The Double*.

2. Kafka, *Diaries*, 27 August, 1916, 2:164

3. Michel Foucault has provided an analysis of power that reworks all economic and political questions. Although his method is completely different, his analysis is not without a certain Kafkaesque resonance. Foucault insists on the segmentarity of power, its contiguity, its immanence in the social field (which means that it is not an interiority of a soul or of a subject along the lines of a superego). He shows that power doesn't work at all by the classic alternative of violence or ideology, persuasion or constraint. See Foucault's *Discipline and Punish*, trans. Alan Sheridan (New York: Pantheon, 1977): the field of immanence and the multiplicity of power in "disciplinary societies."

4. Cited in Wagenbach, *Franz Kafka*, 169.

5. Gustave Janouch, *Conversations*, 174. And for the preceding citations, pp. 102-103, Janouch tells how, one day, under the entrance to the Worker's Insurance offices, Kafka lowered his head, seemed to tremble, and "vigorously crossed himself with a great Roman cross" (p. 102).

6. Janouch, *Conversations*, 143.

7. Ibid., 45: "You say far more about the impressions which things inspire in you than about the things and objects themselves. That is lyrical poetry. You caress the world, instead of grasping it."

8. Similarly, in *The Castle*, Barnabas, comparing "the many portraits that have been done of Klamm," and his supposed appearances, sees differences that are all the more disconcerting in that they are absolutely minimal and indescribable.

## CHAPTER 7. THE CONNECTORS

1. Kafka, *Diaries*, 21 July 1913, 292-93.

2. Kafka, *Diaries*, 29 July 1914, 2:71.

3. Kafka, *The Castle*, trans. Willa and Edwin Muir (New York: Alfred A. Knopf, 1962), 54 (the scene with Frieda).

4. Class struggle already permeates the family and the store at the level of the maids and the employees. This is one of the central themes of Kafka's "The Letter to His Father" (New York: Schocken Books, 1966). One of Kafka's sisters was reproached about her attraction to maids and to country life. The first time that Kafka saw Felice, she had "a bare throat," "an almost broken nose," "a face that wore its emptiness openly," large teeth; he takes her to be a maid (Kafka, *Diaries*, 20 August 1912, 268-69). But also, to be a sister, and a whore. She isn't: like Kafka himself, she is already an important bureaucrat and will end up as a company director. Nonetheless, Kafka will gain secret pleasures from her as a kind of adjustment of the bureaucratic gears or segments.

5. See Max Brod, "Postface to *The Castle*"; Wagenbach, *Kafka par lui-même*, 102-3.

6. One of the models for the artist, or for Titorelli, has to be Oskar Pollak, one of the most mysterious of Kafka's childhood friends. Kafka undoubtedly felt a great love for him, but Pollak quickly got out of it and died at an early age in 1915. He wasn't a painter but a specialist in the Italian Baroque. He had a remarkable competence in a large number of areas that must have intrigued Kafka: architecture, urban cartography, old administrative and commercial books; see Max Brod, *Franz Kafka*, 54-59.

7. Kafka, "The Substitute": "As to the way in which the exclamation and the song were connected, almost all the witnesses had a different opinion, the accuser even pretended that it wasn't the accused but someone else who had sung."

8. Titorelli "was no more questionable as an ally than the lawyer."

9. Michel Carrouges uses the term *bachelor machines* to designate a certain number of fantastic machines described in literature: among them, that of "The Penal Colony." However, we don't accept his interpretation of Kafka's machines (especially in relation to "the law"). The following passages come from a project of Kafka's for a short story on the theme of the bachelor. See Kafka, *Diaries*, 19 July 1910, 22–29.

## CHAPTER 8. BLOCKS, SERIES, INTENSITIES

1. Maurice Blanchot, who has so well analyzed fragmentary writing, is equally adept at noting the force of the continuous in Kafka (even if he interprets it in a negative way and within the theme of the "lack"): see Blanchot, *L'Amitié* (Paris: Gallimard, 1971), 316–319.

2. See Max Brod, *Franz Kafka*, 151 (Brod reproduces here a "life program" that Kafka drew up for himself).

3. Kafka, *Diaries*, 8 October 1917, 2:189.

4. Kafka, "Description of a Struggle," in *Complete Stories*, 15.

5. Kafka writes a letter to his sister Elly that is a sort of counterpart to "The Letter to His Father". (Compare Kafka, *Letters*, 294–97.) Referring to Swift, Kafka opposes the familial animal and the human animal. As a familial animal, the child is caught up in a system of power where the parents "arrogate to themselves the sole right . . . to represent the family." This whole family system consists of the two coexisting poles: lowering one's head and raising one's head ("slavery and tyranny"). The spontaneous life of the child as a human animal lies elsewhere, in a certain deterritorialization. Thus, he must quickly try to leave his familial milieu, as Kafka wanted his nephew Felix to do. Unless the child comes from a poor family in which case "their working-life cannot be kept at a distance from their hut" (there is no being thrown back onto an individual situation; the child is immediately connected to an extraparental social field). But if the child isn't poor, the best thing to do is leave even if the child "returns to his native village, [recognized by no one]. This is the true nature of mother love." This is because the childhood block functioned through the mother.

6. Once again, we should compare him to Proust, who also makes ample use of the two poles of mannerism: worldly mannerism as an art of the faraway, an exaggeration of the phantom-obstacle, and the childhood mannerism as an art of the contiguous (not only are the famous involuntary memories real childhood blocks, but so is the uncertainty of the narrator's age at various points in the text). In other arrangements, the two mannerisms also operate in the work of Holderlin or Kleist.

## CHAPTER 9. WHAT IS AN ASSEMBLAGE?

1. See Brod, *Franz Kafka*, 82.

2. Wagenbach, *Kafka par lui-même*, 82–85. (Wagenbach cites a detailed report by Kafka on the utility of cylindrical spindles in planing-machines).

Index

# Index

Segment, 56, 84; hard, x. See also *Trial, The*
Sephiha, Vidal, 22
Sense, 21
Series, 72–81; proliferation of, 53–63. *See also* Blocks; Proliferation
"Should We Burn Kafka?," xxviii, 47, 96 n3
Signification, 3, 7, 22; orders of, xi–xii. *See also* Sound Sisters, 65
Sobriety, 25, 58; mannerism of, 79; as method, 19
Socialism, 57. *See also Amerika*
Sound, 4–6 *passim*, 28, 51, 65; and deterritorialization, 21
Stalinism, 41, 83
Statement (*Énoncé*), 82, 95 n16
Stories, 34–37, 54. *See also* Machine
Subject, ix, 18, 31, 53, 83; categories of, 18; of enunciation and of statement, 20; in the letters, 30–31. *See also* Doubling; Series

*Tel Quel*, xxiii
"Temptation in the Village," 15
Tensors, 22–23
Thanatos, 36, 59
Theology, xviii
Third International, 75
Topography, 31–32, 73–75. See also *Castle, The*; Maps
Totalities, 85
Trial (*Procés*), *See* Assemblage
*Trial, The*, 5, 11, 40, 43–53 *pasim*, 57,

63–68 *passim*; acquittal in, 72; familial triangle in, 54; film of, 76; law and desire in, 50; mannerism in, 79–80; photos, 4; retriangulation in, 88; segment in, 84; series in, 85; topography in, 73. *See also* Brod, Max; Uyttersprot, Herman
Triangle; familial, 11–14; bureaucratic, 14. *See also* "Metamorphosis, The"; Proliferation; *Trial, The*

Uyttersprot, Herman, 44

Vampirism, 29–30, 32; fear of, 46; in Proust, 34, 94 n4
Vection, xii, xvii, 28
"Verdict, The," 31, 73

Wagenbach, Klaus, 23, 68
"Wedding Preparations," 31
Wegener, Paul, xv, 24
Welles, Orson, 76
Whores, 65
Wiene, Robert, xv, 24
*Wörterflucht*, 26
Writing, 41, 47

Yiddish, 25

Zionism, 19, 92 n6. *See also* Reterritorialization

**Gilles Deleuze** is professor of philosophy at the University of Paris (Vincennes). Among his many books are studies of Kant, Spinoza, and Nietzsche. Some recent translations from Minnesota include: *Kant's Critical Philosophy* (1985) and *Cinema 1: Movement-Image* (1986). Forthcoming from Minnesota is *Cinema 2: Time-Image*.

**Félix Guattari** is a psychoanalyst at the LaBorde clinic and co-author with Gilles Deleuze of *Anti-Oedipus* (Minnesota paperback, 1983) and *A Thousand Plateaus*, forthcoming from Minnesota.

**Dana Polan** is associate professor of film and English at the University of Pittsburgh, and author of *Power and Paranoia: History, Narrative, and the American Cinema, 1940–1950* (Columbia, 1986).

**Réda Bensmaïa** teaches French and comparative literature at the University of Minnesota, and is author of *The Barthes Effect*, forthcoming from Minnesota.